TH
TRADITIO

THE TRADITIONAL CUISINE OF BUNDELKHAND - I

Detailed Recipes in all Cuisine Categories

Prof. RAM NATH MISHRA
Mrs. REKHA MISHRA

FROM THE AUTHORS

Prof. Ramnath Mishra
Mrs. Rekha Mishra

November 10, 2015
Bengaluru

Dear Reader,

Greetings!

These two volumes of the new book *'Bundelkhand's Traditional Cuisine'* may come as surprise to you, as a disruption to *'Encyclopedia of Original Hinduism'*.

The context goes back to incident which took place three years back. I was teaching about the patents under Quality Assurance to the PG students. During discussion on the Geographically Distinct Products, I refered to one Bundeli food dish which is geographically specific to Bundelkhand but not a single student had heard about it, leave alone eating or being cooked at home, in their entire memory.

The fast disappearance of the Traditional Cuisine is taking place all regions of our nation because we are heading to a sort of standardized cuisine.

All regions, in our nation, are rich in culimanary art and have real tasty, healthy and yet very simple dishes, with their own geographically distinctive dishes.

We know this first hand as we had been posted in various regions, during our career, and we learnt some of their cusine ourself, from the friends there. The other friends in those regions taught us about cuisine of their regions.

Some of these dishes are present in today's '*National Standard Menu*' but without giving credit to the region of origin.

The same is true about Bundelkhand.

So when Mrs. Rekha Mishra, my wife, suggested that we must write on priority about the '*Traditional Cuisine of Bundelkhand*', I agreed immediately.

This has resulted in these two volumes of '*Traditional Cuisine of Bundelkhand Region*'

It is hoped that you would relish these original and authentic dishes and pass on the book to the younger ones in the family, serving the intended purpose of this book.

We shall be happy to hear from you, once you have cooked and relished any dish from these three regions.

Personal regards and happy cooking and dining!

Prof. Ram Nath Mishra				Mrs. Rekha Misha
rnmishr@gmail.com

ACKNOWLEDGEMENT

We are indebted to our Didi,
Smt. Anjali Devi Tiwari
(Retd. Lecturer, Junior College, Bhilai Steel Plant)
For her invaluable contribution in providing
Names and details of many age old
But now forgotten recipes of Bundelkhandi cuisine.

DISCLAIMER

In case, one is allergic to or does not like any food ingredient (Grains, Vegetables, Fruits, Spices, Salts, Oils, Ghee or any other ingredient), he / she should not use it. The Oil / Ghee / Vanaspati which suits one's constitution should only be used.

For any new ingredient or the dish, it is advisable that at first, one may prepare (proportionately) small quantity of dish and taste to check that it suits one's constitution and is safe.

Even the quantities of agreeable ingredients, (e.g. Sugar, Jaggery, Spices, Chilies, Souring agents etc.) should also be adjusted to one's taste and tolerance to his / her constitution.

In case of any problem of any kind to anyone caused inadvertently, the authors and the publisher are not responsible / liable for the same.

Prof. Ram Nath MishraMrs. Rekha Mishra

Contents

FROM THE AUTHORS 2
ACKNOWLEDGEMENT 4
DISCLAIMER 5

CHAPTER 1: INTRODUCTION 7

CHAPTER 2: DEFINITIONS & EXPLANATIONS / ENGLISH-HINDI EQUIVALENTS 12
   FLOURS 12
   PULSES / LEGUMES 12
   OILS 13
   SPICES 13
   VEGETABLES 15
   OTHERS 17
   PROCESS 17

CHAPTER 3: BREAD 18
   A. ROTIS 18
   B. PARAATHAA 24
   C. BHARVAA PARATHE (STUFFED PARATHE) 28
   D. POORIE 34
   E. KHAAS POORIEYAA (SPECIAL POORIES) 42
   F. BHATHURAA 44

CHAPTER 4: RICE DISHES 46

CHAPTER 5: SABJIYAA (VEGETABLE PREPARATIONS) 49

CHAPTER 6: DAARE / DAAL (LENTILS AS CURRY) 111

CHAPTER 7: BARI CURRIES 117

CHAPTER 8: BESAN KI SOOKHI SABJIYAA (CHICKPEA FLOUR BASED DRY VEG) 119

CHAPTER 9: DAHI AUR MATHAA KA RASILAA KHAANAA (CURD AND BUTTERMILK CURRIES) 122
   A. BUNDELI KADIS: 122

CHAPTER 1: INTRODUCTION

The Bundelkhand Region:

The Bundelkhand region is spread in Madhya Pradesh and Uttar Pradesh. There are 8 Districts in M.P. which together are named the Bundelkhand Commissionary, with Sagar as headquarter. The 7 Districts are in U.P. and Jhansi is the main city.

The people outside this region know about **Jhansi ki Rani, Laxmi Bai**, the prominent warrior leader of First War of Independence.

The other great leader from this region is (Late) **Sir (Dr.) Hari Singh Gaur**, a leading legal wizard, then practiced at Privy council London, who founded the University of Sagar, with his personal money in 1945 (An University situated on a hill top spread in more than 2000 Acres). Now it is Central University and renamed after him.

About this book: The population of Bundelkhand region is about 2.5 crore. Apart from other things, the Bundelkhandi cuisine stands out with its unique characteristics.

But with the passing time, those dishes are disappearing fast, along with the dishes of other regions in our country, with certain dishes emerging as pan India menu.

These books represent our efforts to preserve their existence for the time when they once again regain the prominence.

Certain characteristics of Bundeli Cuisine:

1. Maximization of use of all food resources:

There is emphasis on the maximization of use of all food resources.

The wild produce like **Ber (Jujube fruits)** are used as:
   i. Consumed as fruits
   ii. Curry is prepared of raw and ripe fruits
   iii. Chatni is made of semi ripe and ripe fruits
   iv. Dried fruits are preserved and use throughout the year as 'Labdo' after boiling

 v. Boiled water of 'Labdo' is used as energy drink
 vi. Dried fruits are preserved in pulverized form called Mirchun and consumed throughout the year.

Or take the case of **Radish**. In this case, the radish is used for:
 i. Salad ingredient
 ii. Curry preparation
 iii. Curry preparation of its leaves
 iv. Chatni preparation
 v. Pickle preparation

Even the lentils are used maximally. Take the case of **Chickpea / Chanaa**, also called Black chanaa. It is used as
 i. As chaat (Boiled in salt water)
 ii. Masala chaat (Boiled in salted water and fried in oil with onion, chilies and garlic)
 iii. As Daal (Accompaniment to Roti and Rice preparations).
 iv. As major ingredient (Fill) of Pooran Poorie and sole ingredient in 'Cheelaa'.
 v. Its flour is used in Multigrain Roti preparations like 'Birraa' or the food like 'Satuaa'.
 vi. Its flour, called Besan, is used in preparation of Kadi (Another accompaniment to Roti and Rice preparations).
 vii. Besan is also used in preparing hundreds of salty Namkeen preparations
 viii. Besan is also used in preparing many sweet preparations.
 ix. Besan is ingredient in scores of curries and other accompaniment dishes.

2. The use of Ghee:
The use of Ghee is preferred over Vanaspati in preparation of the sweets, Paraathaa, Poorie and for garnishing the Roti and Daal (and Baghaar application in Daal). Ghee is very tasty and healthy when consumed in moderation.

3. The use of Jaggery:
Jaggery is the preferred sweetening agent. It is proved now by modern science that white sugar is not healthy but jiggery is.

4. Avoidance or minimal use of spices:

1. The addition of the spices and the souring agents (like tomatoes, lemon juice, Amchur and tamarind paste) are avoided or added minimally in order **to protect and accentuate the original taste of the vegetables as well as to retain their health benefits, legumes, bari or daals.**

5. Novel applications of the cooking processes:
The enhancement of the taste is also achieved by varying the cooking process like roasting and boiling etc.

6. Retaining even bitter taste for health benefits:

For the same reason, the bitterness of Bitter gourd is not removed as these bitters are contributors to heath (So the bitter gourds are neither peeled nor they are treated with salt).

On the other hand the bitterness of green cucumber is removed (as it is not beneficial) in form of foam, by rubbing its both exposed surfaces (by cutting its own head, about half a cm thick piece) against each other.

7. Preference for Green chili over red one:
In cooking the vegetables, green chilies are preferred over red chili powder because of fragrance and taste.

8. The avoidance or the minimal use of souring agents:
The desi (as against hybrid) tomatoes are used in Bundelkhand which have thin film like skin and high content of melic acid (hence they are sourer). So in order to retain the original taste of vegetables legumes, Bari or daals, the tomatoes are added in minimum quantity or avoided altogether.

9. The minimal use of Moyan:
The Moyan is used in nominal amount in dough of Paraathaa or Poorie as the people prefer 'Khari' (Hard / Brittle) type preparation.

10. Chatnis and Pickles galore:

Chatnis:

Consistency: The Chatnis are grinded a bit coarser. This consistency improves the feel in the mouth as well as the retention time.

Minimum ingredients: The chain recipes have minimum ingredients so that the taste and the flavor of the original / main ingredient is retained.

Avoidance of extraneous taste enhancers: As far as possible, the addition of the extraneous taste enhancers and souring agents, is avoided.

The process innovations for taste improvement:
The process innovations like roasting and select spices and / or salts are used to serve the purpose. Even the fruits are used at different stages of growth (like semi ripe and ripe).

The traditional grinding / milling: The Chatnis are grinded using Sil-Lodaa. Both are made of stone. Sil is in form of flat stone of 1.5 feet by 1 foot in size. This Sil is engraved with mini shallow pits to impart the friction when the Lodaa (Pestle) is moved on it with pressure to grind the Chatni contents. In this case, the contents are placed one by one on the Sil and grinded. Finally all pastes are mixed and grinded together.

Thus Chatnis could be prepared using this set of stone grinder or the electrical mixer.

Pickles: Comparatively these chapters contain more recipes because the local people of Bundelkhand have made **innovations** in these fields to get maximum variety (of spicy kind). Again they are appetizer, digestive and cure 'lack of taste'.

In Bundeli pickles, in order **to preserve the original and natural taste of food items**, the whole fruit / vegetable is used.

1. No ingredient is mixed with salt and kept aside to delete the specific taste.

2. The seeds are not removed (whether chili or guava).
One should get the natural taste of the fruit, vegetable or spice which is being pickled.

In Bundelkhand, the **spices are grinded a bit coarser**. This consistency improves the feel in the mouth as well as the retention time.

Again the pickle recipes have **minimum ingredients** so that the taste and the flavor of the original / main ingredient is retained.

As far as possible, the addition of the extraneous taste enhancers and souring agents, the process innovations like roasting and select spices and / or the various salts are used to serve the purpose.

Multigrain: The present Multigrain Flour trend had been the regular culture of Bundelkhand. It does not restrict to **multi-grain flours (Birraa and Satuaa)** but also prevalent in **lentils (two daals cooked together), Khichri** (rice and lentil).

Sweets and dry fruits: In Bundelkhand, Chironji / *Buchanania Latifolia* (The inner seed of Achaar fruit) is the **local dry fruit** and it is very tasty and economical, hence in most sweet preparations, it is used. (But now it costs at par of Almonds).

The options (to suit current taste before graduating to the Original Cuisine): The original recipes got modified with time, so the additional or substitute ingredients in vogue now, have been given as 'Optional ingredients'.

The local produce (Like Chironji): The water chestnuts (Singhaaraa) and the Lotus stem (Muraar) and its fruit (Kamal-gattaa) are cultivated in the ponds as regular crops, hence there are dishes made of these items (Sweets, curry, pickles etc.)

Prepared and Preserved Foods: In some extreme seasons, the vegetables were not available or were prohibitively costly, so the people developed the preserved foods. Some of the examples are Bari (Very popular nationally), Kheechlaa, Kachariyaa and Bijoraa.

CHAPTER 2: DEFINITIONS & EXPLANATIONS / ENGLISH-HINDI EQUIVALENTS

Commonly used ingredients:

FLOURS

S.No.	Name in English	Name in Hindi
1.	Black gram	Urad
2.	Gram / Chickpea	Besan
3.	Green gram	Moong
4.	Maize	Makka
5.	Pearl millet	Baajraa
6.	Rice	Chaaval
7.	Sorghum	Jwaar
8.	Wheat	Gehu
9.	Flour	Aataa
10.	Semolina	Ravaa / Sooji
11.	Water Chestnut	Singhaaraa

PULSES / LEGUMES

S.No.	Name in English	Name in Hindi
1.	Black gram	Urad
2.	Gram / Chickpea	Chanaa
3.	Green gram	Moong
4.	Pigeon pea	Tuar
5.	Bengal gram	Masoor
6.	Chinese beans	Raajmaa
7.	Flat beans	Sem phalli
8.	Garden pea	Matar

OILS

S.No.	Name in English	Name in Hindi
1.	Groundnut	Moong-phalli ka Tel
2.	Sesame / Gingelly	Tili ka Tel
3.	Coconut	Naariyal ka Tel
4.	Mustard	Sarson ka Tel
5.	Sunflower	Soorya-mukhi ka Tel
6.	Safflower	Kardi ka Tel

SPICES

1. DRY SPICES

S.No.	Name in English	Name in Hindi
1.	Mango powder (Raw and dried)	Amchur
2.	Cumin seeds	Jeeraa / Jira
3.	Black Caraway	Shah-Jeeraa
4.	Fenugreek	Methi
5.	Lovage	Ajwain
6.	Celery fruit	Badi Ajwain / Ajmodaa
7.	Star Anise	-
8.	Coriander	Dhaniyaa
9.	Turmeric	Haldi
10.	Mustard	Rai
11.	Asafoetida	Hing
12.	Black Pepper	Kali-mirch
13.	Cinnamon Leaves	Tej-patta
14.	Cinnamon Bark	Daal-chini
15.	Nutmeg	Jaiphal
16.	Mace	Jai-Patri
17.	Red Chili	Laal Mirch

S.No.	Name in English	Name in Hindi
18.	Black Cardamom	Badi or Dondaa Elaaychi
19.	Clove	Laung / Lavang
20.	Poppy Seeds	Khas-khas
21.	Nigelia seeds	Kalongi
22.	Fennel	Saunf
23.	Indian Confectionery	Kokam seeds
24.	Black stone flower	Kalpasi / Patthar ke phool
25.	Saffron	Kesar
26.	Coconut	Nariyal

* Nigelia seeds (Kalongi) should not be given during pregnancy. It could cause abortion.

2. SOURING AGENTS

S.No.	Name in English	Name in Hindi
1.	Tomato**	Tamaatar
2.	Curd (In J & K)	Dahi
3.	Tamarind (In South India)	Imli
4.	Raw Mango powder / flakes (In Central India)	Amchur
5.	Lemon juice	Nimbu-ras

** Tomato is mostly used to impart sourness.

3. FRESH SPICES

S.No.	Name in English	Name in Hindi
1.	Green Chili	Hari Mirch
2.	Ginger	Adrak
3.	Garlic	Lahsun
4.	Onion	Pyaaz
5.	Coriander leaves	Dhaniya Patti
6.	Mint leaves	Pudina Patti

| 7. | Curry leaves | Curry Patta |

4. FRESH HERBS

S.No.	Name in English	Name in Hindi
1.	Spring onion	Haraa Pyaaz
2.	Holy Basil	Tulsi / Tulasi
3.	Celery	Sileri
4.	Lettuce leaves	Salad ki patti

5. SPECIAL SALTS

S.No.	Name in English	Name in Hindi
1.	Black salt	Kaalaa Namak
2.	Rock salt	Sendhaa Namak

VEGETABLES

1. FRUITS & VEGETABLES

S.No.	Name in English	Name in Hindi
1.	Ash gourd	Pethaa / Kumharaa
2.	Bitter gourd	Karelaa
3.	Ribbed gourd	Turai
4.	Sponge gourd	Gilki / Phadkuli
5.	Snake gourd	Chacheraa
6.	Brinjal	Baigan / Bhataa
7.	Eggplant / White round Brinjal	Safed Baigan
8.	Capsicum	Shimla mirch
9.	Carrots	Gaajar
10.	Cauliflower	Phool-Gobi
11.	Corn	Maize Makka
12.	Colocasia	Arabi / Ghuiyaa

13.	Cucumber	Kakri / Kheeraa
14.	Drumsticks	Mungaa / Kons
15.	Gherkins	Kundru / Tundli
16.	Lemon	Nimbu
17.	Green peas	Haraa Matar
18.	Ladies Finger / Okra	Bhindi
19.	Mango (Raw)	Kachchaa Aam
20.	Mushroom	-
21.	Pumpkin	Kumharaa / Kaddu
22.	Tomatoes	Tamaatar

2. LEAFY VEGETABLES

S.No.	Name in English	Name in Hindi
1.	Amaranth Leaves	Laal Bhaaji / Marsaa
2.	Lambs Leaves	Bathuaa Bhaaji
3.	Fenugreek Leaves	Methi Bhaaji
4.	Prickly Amaranthus	Chaulai Bhaaji
5.	Spinach	Paalak Bhaaji

3. BEANS VEGETABLES:

S.No.	Name in English	Name in Hindi
1.	Broad Beans	Papdi
2.	Cluster Beans	Guar Phalli / Gawar Phalli
3.	French beans	Fansi phalli
4.	Beans	Sem phalli

4. ROOTS & TUBERS VEGETABLES

S.No.	Name in English	Name in Hindi
1.	Beet Root	Chukandar
2.	Colocasia	Arabi / Ghuiyaa
3.	Potato	Aaloo

4.	Sweet Potato	Shaklaa
5.	Yam	Sooran
6.	Radish	Mooraa / Mooli
7.	Turnip	Shalgam

OTHERS

S.No.	Name in English	Name in Hindi
1.	Vinegar	Sirkaa
2.	Peel / Rind	Chhilkaa
3.	Betel leaves	Paan
4.	Areca nut	Supaari

PROCESS

Soak overnight: 9-12 Hours soaking in water at ambient temperature

No re-heating of oils / Ghee / Vanaspati

The fats and oils should be taken in measured quantity for heating. Once heated in the process, they should not be re-heated again.

These already heated fats and oils could be used in products where their direct heating is not required.

CHAPTER 3: BREAD

A. ROTIS

1. SAADI ROTI

Ingredients:
- i. Wheat flour — 2 Cups
- ii. Water — as required
- iii. Ghee *(For garnishing)* — as required

Process:
- i. The water is mixed in the flour and it is kneaded to make dough.
- ii. The dough is divided in to small Lois / Balls.
- iii. The Lois are rolled in to pancakes.
- iv. The pancakes are roasted on the hot Tawaa first then in the direct fire.
- v. The Rotis are garnished with Ghee on upper side.

2. SINGHAARAA KI ROTI (ROTI OF WATER CHESTNUT FLOUR)

All the ingredients and the process remain same as above (Saadi Roti) except that Water chestnut flour is used in place of wheat flour.

3. JAU / JAVAA ROTI (ROTI OF BARLEY FLOUR)

All the ingredients and the process remain same as above (Saadi Roti) except that Barley flour is used in place of wheat flour.

4. GEHU AUR JAVAA KI ROTI (WHEAT AND BARLEY FLOURS)

This is another Multi-grain (Two grains) flour and its products i.e. Roti, Poorie and Paraathaa.

* **Sufficient for 2 persons.**

Ingredients of Birraa flour:
- i. Wheat

    ii. Barley

Process:
Both the grains are mixed and milled together and mixed again to get the homogeneous flour.

Ingredients of Birraa Roti:
   i. Gehu-javaa flour   500 Gm
   ii. Water   as required
   iii. Ghee   as required
   (For garnishing)

Process:
   i. The water is mixed in the flour and it is kneaded to make dough.
   ii. The dough is divided in to small Lois / Balls.
   iii. The Lois are rolled in to pancakes.
   iv. The pancakes are roasted on the Tawaa first then in the fire.
   v. The Gehu-javaa Rotis are garnished with Ghee on upper side.

5. JUARI ROTI (SORGHUM ROTI)

* Sufficient for 4-5 persons

Ingredients:

i. Sorghum flour   1 Kg

ii. Hot Water   as required*
(to make the soft dough)

* Sorghum requires more water than wheat flour.

Optional ingredient:

Moyan (Oil) could be used to make the Rotis softer.

Process:

i. The flour is kneaded with hot water to make the dough.

ii. The big Loi / Balls are prepared from the dough.

iii. Some water is place on one palm and both the hands are rubbed so that they become wet.

iv. A Loi / Ball is placed on one palm and pressed with other to flatten it.

v. The flattened ball is rotated between the wet hands and pressed regularly.
vi. The palms are wetted repeatedly in this process.
vii. Once it gains the adequate size (still quite thick, known as Motaa Tikkad), it is baked on the Tavaa first and then on the open fire.

The Juari Roti is served with Coriander Chatni. It is also served with Brinjal Bhartaa and Tomato Chatni.

6. JUARI & GEHU KI ROTI (SORGHUM & WHEAT ROTI)

Sufficient for 4-5 persons.

The Juari Rotis tend to crack despite care. When 25% Wheat flour and 75% Sorghum (Jvaar) flours are mixed, the problem of cracking is no longer faced. The dough Loi / Balls could be rolled also as against making by rotating between the hands / palms.

Ingredients:
  i. Sorghum flour   750 Gm
  ii. Wheat flour   250 Gm
  iii. Hot water   as required

Optional ingredient: Moyan (Oil) could be used to make the Rotis softer.

Process:
  i. Both the flours are mixed together and kneaded with hot water to make the dough.
  ii. The small Loi / Balls are prepared from the dough.
  iii. The Loi / Balls are rolled in to Rotis.
  iv. Once it gains the adequate size, it is baked on the Tavaa first and then on the open fire.

Serve: As per Juari Roti

7. BIRRAA ROTI (ROTI OF BIRRAA)

This is earlier Multi-grain (Two grains) flour and its products i.e. Roti and Poorie.

* **Sufficient for 2 persons.**

Ingredients of Birraa flour:
i. Wheat
ii. Chickpea (Whole)

Process:
Both the grain are mixed and milled together and mixed again to get the homogeneous flour.

Ingredients of Birraa Roti:
i.	Birraa flour	500 Gm
ii.	Water	as required
iii.	Ghee *(For garnishing)*	as required

Process:
i. The water is mixed in the flour and it is kneaded to make dough.
ii. The dough is divided in to small Lois / Balls.
iii. The Lois are rolled in to pancakes.
iv. The pancakes are roasted on the Tawaa first then in the fire.
v. The Birraa Rotis are garnished with Ghee on upper side.

8. METHI ROTI (ROTIS WITH FENUGREEK LEAVES)

Ingredients:
i.	Wheat flour	2 Cups
ii.	Water	as required
iii.	Fenugreek leaves *(Finely minced)*	1 Cup
iv.	Green chili	1 Tbs
v.	Salt	to taste
vi.	Ghee *(For garnishing)*	as required
vii.	Water	as required

Process:
i. The finely minced fenugreek leaves, grated green chilies and salt are mixed in the wheat flour.
ii. Water is added in the flour and it is kneaded to make dough.
iii. The dough is divided in to small Lois / Balls
iv. The Lois are rolled in to pancakes.

v. The pancakes are roasted on the hot Tawaa first then in the direct fire.
vi. The Methi Rotis are garnished with Ghee on upper side.

9. PAALAK ROTI (ROTIS WITH SPINACH LEAVES)

All the ingredients and the process remain same as above (Methi Roti) except that spinach leaves are used in place of fenugreek leaves.

10. BHAAT ROTI (COOKED RICE IN WHEAT FLOUR)

All the ingredients and the process remain same as above (Methi Roti) except that the cooked rice (Bhaat) is used in place of fenugreek leaves.

11. GAANKAR - BHARTAA (ROASTED WHEAT FLOUR CAKES & ROASTED MASHED BRINJAL PULP)

* Sufficient for 4 persons.

As the name indicates, this is combo dish of Gaankar and Brinjal Bhataa.

11A. GAANKAR (ROASTED WHEAT FLOUR CAKES):

Ingredients:

i. Wheat flour   1 Kg

ii. Water to make dough

Process:

i. The flour is kneaded with water to make the dough.
ii. The small Loi / Balls are prepared from the dough and are slightly flattened by applying force between the palms..
iii. The completely dried cow dung fuel-cakes are placed on iron plate and lit.
iv. When the smoke and flames are over and only the burning fuel-cakes remain, then these flattish balls are inserted between the red ambers so that they are baked from all the sides.

(In the outdoor picnic, this fire is arranged in the open ground which is clean and even).

v. These baked / cooked balls are taken out of fire, couple of times, with the aid of an iron rod / wet wooden stick, to check the state of cooking. If they are found not sufficiently cooked, they are re-inserted in the burning fuel-cakes.

vi. They are removed from the fire when they are cooked and cleaned with rough, clean cloth.

vii. They are pierced with needle at multiple places on all sides and dipped in the molten Ghee.

They are **served** with Brinjal Bhartaa (as given under 'Dry Vegetables') and Kothambir Chatni.

11B. BHOONJE BHATE KA BHARTAA (ROASTED MASHED BRINJAL PULP)

* Sufficient for 4 persons.

This is very tasty and healthy dish.

Ingredients:

i.	Brinjal	500 Gm
	(Big size, Green or Violet)	
ii.	Asafoetida	¼ Ts
iii.	Mustard seeds	¼ Ts.
iv.	Green Chilies	1 Tbs
v.	Kothambir	1 Tbs
vi.	Salt	to taste
vii.	Rock salt	to taste

Process:

This process is recommended by Ayurveda and states that this non-fried dish alleviates all the vitiated Doshas.

i. Several holes are made in the flesh of Brinjal on all sides and asafoetida is inserted in each hole.

ii. The Brinjal is placed on direct fire for roasting. (A wire mesh may be placed on fire to avoid charring of Brinjal, both surface and flesh).

iii. After due roasting, the Brinjal is removed, cleaned and washed. Then the surface peel is removed.

iv. The flesh is collected, beaten to make uniform consistency. This is Bhartaa.

v. All the ingredients (# iii to vii) are mixed with Bhartaa and it is beaten again to make it homogeneous in taste and consistency.

The Bhoonje Bhataa ka Bhartaa is ready to be served along with Gaakar. It also goes well with other dishes of Rotis.

11C. TALAA BHARTAA (FRIED BHARTAA)

Ingredients & process before the addition of spices remain the same.

Further processing:

The oil is heated in the deep frying pan and all the above spices are added and fried.

Bhartaa is also added to it and mixed thoroughly.

Optional Ingredients: Garlic, Ginger and Onion.

B. PARAATHAA

In Bundelkhand, the Moyan is used in nominal amount in dough of Paraathaa or Poorie as the people prefer 'Khari' (Hard / Brittle) type preparation.

1. SADA PARATHA (PLAIN PARATHA):

Ingredients:
  i. Wheat flour   2 Cups
 ii. Water   as required
iii. Ghee   as required

Process:

i. The Moyan is mixed in the flour, then it is kneaded with water to make dough.
　　ii. The dough is divided in to small Lois / Balls.
　　iii. The Lois are rolled in to pancakes.
　　iv. These pancakes are partially roasted on a heated fry pan / Tavaa, then Ghee is added from the periphery for shallow frying. Then it is turned over and other side is also fried with application of Ghee in the same way.

2. JAU / JAVAA PARAATHAA (PARAATHAA OF BARLEY FLOUR)

All the ingredients and the process remain same as above (Saadaa Paraathaa) except that Barley flour is used in place of wheat flour.

3. SINGHAARAA KA PARAATHAA (PARATHA OF WATER CHESTNUT FLOUR)

All the ingredients and the process remain same as above (Saadaa Paraathaa) except that Water chestnut flour is used in place of wheat flour.

4. AJWAIN PARATHA (LOVAGE PARATHA)

These Paraathaa are highly appetizing and digestive in nature.

Sufficient for 2 persons.

Ingredients:

　　i. Wheat flour　　　　　　500 Gm
　　ii. Water　　　　　　　　as required
　　iii. Lovage (Ajwain)　　　　½ Ts
　　iv. Ghee (Moyan)　　　　　3 Tbs
　　　(For surface frying)

Optional ingredient:

If desired, then Maida could be used in place of Wheat flour and Vanaspati or Oil could be used in place of Ghee.

Process:

i. The lovage is added to the wheat flour and mixed.

i. The Ghee (Moyan) is added to this flour and mixed thoroughly.

ii. The water is added, as required and flour is kneaded thoroughly to make soft dough.

iii. The small Loi / Balls are prepared from the dough.

iv. The Loi / Ball is rolled in to pancake, applying Ghee as required in the rolling process.

v. The pancakes are shallow fried on a frying pan in Ghee.

4A. MAIDAA AJWAIN PARAATHAA (SPICED PARAATHAA OF REFINED WHEAT FLOUR)

Maida is used in place of wheat flour.

5. MASALA PARATHA (MULTI- SPICE PARATHA)

* Sufficient for 2 persons.

Ingredients:

i.	Wheat flour	500 Gm
ii.	Water	as required
iii.	Kothambir*	3 Tbs
iv.	Green Chilies*	3 Tbs or to taste
v.	Salt	to taste
vi.	Lovage (Ajwain)	1 Ts
vii.	Special Garam Masala	2 Ts

* Finely minced

Optional ingredient:

If desired, then Maida could be used in place of Wheat flour and Vanaspati or Oil could be used in place of Ghee.

Process:

i. The lovage, salt and special garam masala are added to the wheat flour and mixed.
ii. The finely minced Kothambir and the green Chilis are also added to this flour and mixed.
iii. The Ghee (Moyan) is added to this flour and mixed thoroughly.
iv. The water is added, as required and flour is kneaded thoroughly to make soft dough.
v. The small Loi / Balls are prepared from the dough.
vi. The Loi / Ball is rolled in to pancake, applying Ghee as required in the rolling process.
vii. The pancakes are shallow fried on a frying pan in Ghee.

These Spiced Paraathaa are best eaten as such or with Chatni / Pickle of one's choice.

5A. MAIDA MASALA PARATHA (SPICED PARATHA OF REFINED WHEAT FLOUR)

Maida is used in place of wheat flour.

6. BIRRAA PARATHA (PARATHA OF BIRRAA)

Birraa flour is prepared as detailed under Birra Roti.

Sufficient for 2 persons.

Ingredients:

i.	Birraa flour	500 Gm
ii.	Lovage (Ajwain)	1 Ts
iii.	Green chilies	2 Tbs
iv.	Kothambir	1 Tbs
v.	Ghee as moyan 2 Tbs	
vi.	Water	as required
vii.	Ghee for shallow frying	as required

Optional ingredient:
Oil could be used in place of Ghee.

Process:

i. The flour is taken in a Paraat.
ii. The lovage seeds are mixed in the flour.
iii. The finely minced green chilies and Kothambir are also mixed in the flour.
iv. The moyan is also mixed in the flour.
v. The water is mixed in the flour and it is kneaded to make dough.
vi. The dough is divided in to small Lois / Balls.
vii. The Lois are rolled in to pancakes.
viii. The pancakes are shallow fried on the frying pan.
ix. After one side is done, the Paraathaa are turned over and fried. Some amount of Ghee is added from the sides.

7. GEHU AUR JAVAA KA PARAATHAA (PARATHA OF WHEAT AND BARLEY FLOURS)

They are prepared in the same way as Birraa Ka Paraathaa, substituting Birraa four with Gehu-Javaa flour.

C. BHARVAA PARATHE (STUFFED PARATHE)

The stuffed Paraathaas involve three steps;
 i. Preparation of the 'Stuffing Mix'.
 ii. Preparation of dough / pancakes.
 iii. Stuffing the mix and preparation of 'Stuffed Paraathaas'.

Optional ingredients in all 8 'Stuffed Parathas':
 i. Maida could be used in place of wheat flour.
 ii. Oil or Vanaspati could be used in place of Ghee.

The step i vary in every recipe but step ii and iii remain the same. Accordingly, in the first recipe all three steps have been detailed and only step i has been detailed in remaining 7 recipes.

* Sufficient for 2-3 persons

1. AALOO PARATHE (POTATO STUFFED PARATHE)

(A). Preparation of the 'Stuffing Mix'.
Ingredients:

i.	Potatoes *(Boiled, peeled, mashed)*	1 Cup
ii.	Green chilies	1 Tbs or to taste
iii.	Ginger	2 Ts
iv.	Garlic	2 Ts
v.	Kothambir	1 Tbs
vi.	Cumin seeds *(Roasted & ground)*	1 Ts
vii.	Turmeric powder	½ Ts
viii.	Special Garam Masala	½ Ts
ix.	Salt	to taste
x.	Water	as required

Process:
1. The potatoes are boiled in water, cooled, peeled and mashed. Ingredients # ii, iii and iv are grated.
2. Kothambir is minced.
3. Cumin seeds are roasted and ground.
4. All these and other spices are added and mixed in the mashed potatoes.
5. The salt is also added.
6. The 'Stuffing Mix' is ready for use.

(B.) Preparation of dough / pancakes.
Ingredients:

i.	Wheat flour	2 Cups
ii.	Water	as required
iii.	Salt	to taste
iv.	Ghee	as required

Process:
i. The Moyan is mixed in the flour. Salt is also added and then it is kneaded with water to make dough.
ii. The dough is divided in to small Lois / Balls.
iii. The Lois are rolled in to pancakes (Triangular or round), adding Ghee on the surface, as needed.

(C.) Stuffing the mix and preparation of 'Stuffed Paraathaa'.

i. The requisite quantity (for one Paraathaa) of the 'Stuffing Mix' (as prepared above) is taken and placed in the center of the pancake.
ii. The pancake is folded from all sides, enveloping the 'Stuffing Mix'.
iii. This round ball like filled Loi is rolled again in to a shorter pancake (Triangular or round). The rolling pressure should be controlled to avoid rupturing the pancake and spilling out of the 'Stuffing Mix'.
iv. These pancakes are partially roasted on a heated fry pan / Tavaa, then Ghee is added from the periphery for shallow frying. When it becomes golden brown, it is turned over and other side is also fried with application of Ghee in the same way.

The Stuffed Paraathaa is ready to be served.

2. GOBHI PARAATHE (CAULIFLOWER STUFFED PARAATHE):

i. Preparation of the 'Stuffing Mix'.
Ingredients:

i.	Cauliflower (Chopped fine)	2 Cup
ii.	Red chili powder	1 Ts or to taste
iii.	Ginger	2 Ts
iv.	Garlic	2 Ts
v.	Cumin seeds (Roasted and ground)	1 Ts
vi.	Turmeric powder	½ Ts
vii.	Special Garam Masala	½ Ts
viii.	Salt	to taste
ix.	Water	as required

Process:
1. The Cauliflower is chopped fine.
2. Ingredients # iii and iv are grated.
3. Cumin seeds are roasted and ground.

4. All these and other spices are added and mixed in the Cauliflower.
5. The salt is also added.
6. The 'Stuffing Mix' is ready for use.

Step ii and iii are same as in case of recipe of 'Potato Stuffed Paraathaa'.

3. AALOO METHI PARAATHE (POTATO FENUGREEK LEAVES STUFFED PARAATHE)

(A) Preparation of the 'Stuffing Mix'
Ingredients:

1.	Potatoes (Boiled, peeled, mashed)	1 Cup
2.	Fenugreek leaves (Chopped and lightly boiled)	1 Cup
3.	Ginger	2 Ts
4.	Garlic	2 Ts
5.	Red chili powder	1 Tbs
6.	Cumin seeds (Roasted & ground)	1 Ts
7.	Turmeric powder	½ Ts
8.	Special Garam Masala	½ Ts
9.	Salt	to taste
10.	Water	as required

Process:
1. The potatoes are boiled in water, cooled, peeled and mashed. The fenugreek leaves are chopped and lightly boiled. Both are mixed together.
2. Ingredients # iii and iv are grated.
3. Cumin seeds are roasted and ground.
4. All these and other spices are added in the potatoes fenugreek mix. The salt is also added.
   The 'Stuffing Mix' is ready for use.

Step (B) and (C) are same as in case of recipe of 'Potato Stuffed Paraathaa'.

4. PATTAA GOBHI PARAATHE (CABBAGE STUFFED PARAATHE)

All ingredients and process is same as that of 'Stuffed Cauliflower Paraathaa' except that cauliflower is substituted by cabbage.

5. KACHOOMAR PARAATHE (RADISH AND TOMATO CHATNI STUFFED PARAATHE)

i. Preparation of the 'Stuffing Mix i.e. Kachoomar Chatni'.
Ingredients:

i.	Radish (Medium size)	3
ii.	Tomato (Big size and firm)	2
iii.	Lemon Juice	2 Ts
iv.	Green chilies (Minced)	1 Tbs or to taste
v.	Salt	to taste

Optional ingredients:
Rock salt and Black salt could be added to taste.

Process:
i. The radishes are cleaned and peeled lightly to remove the minute roots. They are grated.
ii. Tomatoes are also grated, resulting in pieces and juice.
iii. Both ingredients, green chilies, salt and lemon juice are added together and mixed well.

The tasty Kachoomar Chatni is ready.

Step ii and iii are same as in case of recipe of 'Potato Stuffed Paraathaas'.

6. PAALAK PARAATHE (SPINACH STUFFED PARAATHE)

i. Preparation of the 'Stuffing Mix'.
Ingredients:

i.	Spinach leaves (Chopped fine)	2 Cup
ii.	Red chili powder	1 Ts or to taste
iii.	Ginger	2 Ts
iv.	Garlic	2 Ts
v.	Cumin seeds (Roasted & ground)	1 Ts
vi.	Turmeric powder	½ Ts
vii.	Salt	to taste
viii.	Water	as required

Process:
1. The Spinach leaves are chopped fine.
2. Ingredients # iii and iv are grated.
3. Cumin seeds are roasted and ground.
4. All these and other spices are added and mixed in the Cauliflower.
5. The salt is also added. The 'Stuffing Mix' is ready for use.

Step ii and iii are same as in case of recipe of 'Potato Stuffed Paraathaas'.

7. METHI PARAATHE (FENUGREEK LEAVES STUFFED PARAATHE)

All ingredients and process is same as that of 'Stuffed Spinach Paraathaa' except that spinach leaves are substituted by Fenugreek leaves.

8. LAAL BHAAJI PARAATHE (AMARANTHUS STUFFED PARAATHE)

All ingredients and process is same as that of 'Stuffed Spinach Paraathaa' except that spinach leaves are substituted by Amaranthus leaves.

D. POORIE

In Bundelkhand, the moyan is used in nominal amount in dough of Paraathaa or Poorie as the people prefer 'Khari' (Hard / Brittle) type preparation.

1. SAADI POORIE (PLAIN POORIE)

Ingredients:
- i. Wheat flour — 2 Cups
- ii. Water — as required
- iii. Ghee — as required

Process:
- i. The Moyan is mixed in the flour, then it is kneaded with water to make dough.
- ii. The dough is divided in to small Lois / Balls.
- iii. The Lois are rolled in to pancakes.
- iv. The pancakes are deep fried in the heated Ghee in a deep fry pan.

2. RAJGIRAA KI POORIE

All the ingredients and the process remain same as above (Saadi Poorie) except that water chestnut flour is used in place of wheat flour.

3. JAU / JAVAA POORIE (POORIE OF BARLEY FLOUR)

All the ingredients and the process remain same as above (Saadi Poorie) except that Barley flour is used in place of wheat flour.

4. GEHU AUR JAVAA KI POORIE (POORIE OF WHEAT AND BARLEY FLOURS)

They are prepared in the same way as Birraa Ki Poorie, substituting Birraa four with Gehu-Javaa flour.

5. SINGHAARAA KI POORIE (POORIE OF WATER CHESTNUT FLOUR)

All the ingredients and the process remain same as above (Saadi Poorie) except that Water chestnut flour is used in place of wheat flour.

6. AJWAIN POORIE (LOVAGE POORIE)

The ingredients / optional ingredients and the process is similar to the 'Ajwain Paraathaa' (Recipe under the heading 'Paraathaa') except that 'Ajwain Poories' are DEEP FRIED instead of shallow frying.

7. DAAR BHARI POORIE (TODAY'S POORAN-POORIE)

These two preparations are festival preparations and enjoy wide popularity.

These preparations are two stages process.

a. The filling content:

The Sweet Pooran-Poorie has sweet content and Salty Pooran-Poorie has salty content

b. The covering pancake:

This is generally prepared of wheat flour. But Maida is also being used instead.

7A. MEETHI DAAR BHARI POORIE (TODAY'S POORAN-POORIE - SWEET)

The literal English translation of the Bundeli name of this dish would be "Poorie stuffed with sweet lentil".

* **Sufficient for 2 persons.**

a. The filling content:

Ingredients:

i.	Chickpea / Gram *(Chana Daal)*	500 Gm
ii.	Water	as required
iii.	Ghee	100 ml (approx.)
iv.	Sugar	250 Gm (approx.)
v.	Coconut powder	70 Gm
vi.	Cardamom *(Crushed)*	10
vii.	Chironji *(Buchanania latifolia)*	70 Gm

Process:

i. The Chickpea *(Chana Daal)* is soaked in sufficient water and left overnight. The boiling is avoided to avoid cooking.
ii. It is spread on a clean cloth sheet and air-dried.
iii. The dried Daal is pulverized in a mixer.
iv. Ghee is heated in a Deep frying pan / frying pan and this powdered Daal is added in hot Ghee with constant mixing.
v. Lumps formation should be avoided. It is continuously fried with stirring till it starts becoming a single lump.
vi. The coconut powder is added and mixed thoroughly.
vii. Chironjis are added and mixed thoroughly.
viii. Cardamoms are also added and mixed thoroughly.

This content mix is stored securely till the covering pancakes are prepared.

b. The covering pancake:
Ingredients:

i.	Wheat flour	500 Gm
ii.	Water	as required
iii.	Ghee (Moyan)	3 Tbs
iv.	Ghee	as required (For surface frying)

Optional ingredient:
i. Black gram, green gram and peas are also used in place of chickpea.
ii. If desired, then Maida could be used in place of Wheat flour and Vanaspati or Oil could be used in place of Ghee.

Process:
i. The Ghee (Moyan) is added to the flour and mixed thoroughly.
ii. The water is added, as required and flour is kneaded thoroughly to make a soft dough.
iii. The small Loi / Balls are prepared from the dough.
iv. The Loi / Ball is rolled in to pancake, applying Ghee as required in the rolling process.
v. The pancakes are air dried for 10 minutes.

The 'filling content' and frying:
i. Then the 'Filling Content' from step 'a' is taken and the adequate quantity is filled in each pancake.
ii. A drop of water is applied on the circular edge of the pancake and it folded from all sides and pressed to seal to form a Loi / Ball/ Ball again.
iii. This 'filled' Loi / Ball is rolled again to form a pancake.
iv. The pancakes are shallow fried in Ghee on a frying pan like a Paraathaa.

The hot Meethi Daar Bhari Poories are served with Chatni / pickle of choice or it eaten by itself.

7B. MASALA DAAR BHARI POORIE (TODAY'S POORAN-POORIE – SALTY / KACHORI)

The literal English translation of the Bundeli name of this dish would be "Poorie stuffed with spicy lentil".

* Sufficient for 2 persons.

a. The filling content:

Ingredients:

i.	Chickpea / Gram *(Chana Daal)*	500 Gm
ii.	Water	as required
iii.	Oil	100 ml (approx.)
iv.	Salt	to taste
v.	Lovage *(Ajwain)*	1 Ts
vi.	Green Chillies	to taste
vii.	Cumin seeds	2 Ts
viii.	Hing	¼ Ts

Optional Ingredient:

i. Black gram, green gram and peas are also used in place of chickpea.

ii. If desired, then Maida could be used in place of Wheat flour and Vanaspati or Oil could be used in place of Ghee.

iii. Garlic (2Ts) and Ginger (2Ts) are also used in some parts.

Process:

i. The Chickpea (Chana Daal) is soaked in sufficient water and left overnight. The boiling is avoided to avoid cooking.

ii. It is spread on a clean cloth sheet and air-dried.

iii. The dried Daal is pulverized in a mixer.

iv. Oil is heated in a Deep frying pan / frying pan and this powdered Daal is added in hot oil with constant mixing.

v. Lumps formation should be avoided. It is continuously fried with stirring till it starts becoming a single lump.

vi. The Salt is added and mixed thoroughly.

vii. Lovage and Cumin powder are added and mixed thoroughly.

viii. viii. Hing is added followed by green Chili s and mixed thoroughly.

ix. The optional ingredients could be added at this stage.

This content mix is stored securely till the covering pancakes are prepared.

b. The covering pancake:

Ingredients:

i.	Wheat flour	500 Gm
ii.	Water	as required
iii.	Oil *(Moyan)*	3 Tbs
iv.	Oil *(For surface frying)*	as required

Optional Ingredient:

If desired, then Maida could be used in place of Wheat flour.

Process:

i. The Oil (Moyan) is added to the flour and mixed thoroughly.

ii. The water is added, as required and flour is kneaded thoroughly to make soft dough.

iii. The small Loi / Balls are prepared from the dough.

iv. The Loi / Ball is rolled in to pancake, applying oil as required in the rolling process.

v. The pancakes are air dried for 10 minutes.

The 'filling content' and frying:

i.		Then the 'Filling Content' from step 'a' is taken and the adequate quantity is filled in each pancake.
ii.		A drop of water is applied on the circular edge of the pancake and it folded from all sides and pressed to seal to form a Loi / Ball/ Ball again.
iii.		This 'filled' Loi / Ball is rolled again to form a pancake.
iv.		The pancakes are shallow fried in oil on a frying pan like a Paraathaa.

The hot Masala Daar Bhari Poories are served with Chatni / pickle of choice or it eaten by itself.

8. MASALA POORIE (MIXED LEAFY VEGETABLES AND SPICES POORIE)

* **Sufficient for 2 persons.**

Ingredients:

i.	Wheat flour	500 Gms
ii.	Water	as required
iii.	Spinach leaves*	3Tbs
iv.	Fenugreek leaves*	3Tbs
v.	Prickly Amaranth* Chaulai leaves	3Tbs
vi.	Kothambir*	3Tbs
vii.	Green Chilies*	3 Tbs or to taste
viii.	Salt	to taste
ix.	Lovage *(Ajwain)*	1Ts
x.	Special Garam Masala	2Ts

* *Finely minced*

Optional Ingredient:

If desired, then Maida could be used in place of Wheat flour and Vanaspati or Oil could be used in place of Ghee.

Process:

i. The lovage, salt and special garam masala are added to the wheat flour and mixed.
ii. The finely minced Kothambir and the green Chilies are also added to this flour and mixed.
iii. All the three leafy vegetables (finely minced) are also added and mixed thoroughly.
iv. The Ghee (Moyan) is added to this flour and mixed thoroughly.
v. The water is added, as required and flour is kneaded thoroughly to make soft dough.
vi. The small Loi / Balls are prepared from the dough.
vii. The Loi / Ball is rolled in to pancake, applying Ghee as required in the rolling process.
viii. The pancakes are deep fried in a Deep frying pan in Ghee.

These Spiced Paraathaas are best eaten as such or with Chatni / Pickle / Curry of one's choice.

9. BIRRAA KI POORIE

The Birraa Poories ingredients and process is like Birra Roti (Recipe under subject heading 'Roti') except that

i. Moyan is added in the flour before kneading
ii. They are deep fried in Ghee or oil instead of roasting.

10. PAKE KELE KI POORIE (POORIE WITH RIPE BANANA)

All the ingredients and the process remain same as above (Saadi Poorie) except that one ripe banana pulp is added for each 2 cups of wheat flour. Adequate water is added during kneading to get softness of the dough.

11. SABOO-DAANAA KI POORIE (SAGO POORIE)

* **Sufficient for 2 persons.**

Ingredients:

i.	Wheat flour	2 Cups
ii.	Sago *(Saboo-daanaa)*	1 Cup
iii.	Ghee as moyan	2 Tbs
iv.	For deep frying	as required
v.	Cumin seeds	¼ Ts
vi.	Red chili powder	¼ Ts
vii.	Special Garam Masala	½ Ts
viii.	Water	as required

Optional ingredients:
   i. Chaat masala could be used in place of Special Garam Masala.
   ii. Oil could be used in place of Ghee.

Process:
   i. Soak the Sago in water for 1 to 2 hours or till it becomes soft.
   ii. It is placed in a muslin cloth and hanged so that the extra water is drained off.
   iii. The soft sagoes are mixed with flour and kneaded.
   iv. Cumin seeds, red chili powder and Special Garam Masala are added in the semi-finished dough and mixed thoroughly. The mix is kneaded well.
   v. Dough is allowed to stand for 45 minutes undisturbed.
   vi. The small Loi / Balls are prepared from the dough.
   vii. The Lois / Balls are rolled in to pancake, applying Ghee as required in the rolling process.
   viii. The pancakes are deep fried in the Ghee, in Deep frying pan.

The Saboo-daanaa ki Poories are ready to be served.

E. KHAAS POORIEYAA (SPECIAL POORIES)

1. KACHCHE DHANIYAA CHATNI KI MASAALAA POORIE (SPICED POORIE WITH RAW AND GREEN CORIANDER SEEDS CHATNI)

[i.] KACHCHE DHANIYAA CHATNI PREPARATION:

Ingredients:

i.	Green immature coriander seeds	½ Cup
ii.	Green chilies	4
iii.	Cumin seeds	½ Ts
iv.	Salt	To taste
v.	Water	1- 1½ Tbs

Process:
i. The green chilies are cut in small pieces.
ii. The Green immature coriander seeds, the green chili pieces and the salt are placed in the mixer bowl and grinded together.
iii. If need be, to aid grinding or adjust consistency, water could be added.

[ii.] POORIE PREPARATION:

Ingredients:
i.	Wheat flour	2 Cups
ii.	Chatni from [i.]	
iii.	Water	as required
iv.	Ghee	as required

Process:
i. The Moyan is mixed in the flour.
ii. Chatni is added and mixed.
iii. Then it is kneaded with water to make dough.
iv. The dough is divided in to small Lois / Balls.
v. The Lois are rolled in to pancakes.
vi. The pancakes are deep fried in the heated Ghee in a deep fry pan.

2. METHI BHAAJI POORIE (POORIE WITH FENUGREEK LEAVES)

Ingredients:
i.	Wheat flour	2 Cups
ii.	Water	as required

iii.	Fenugreek leaves *(Finely minced)*	1 Cup
iv.	Salt	to taste
v.	Ghee *(For garnishing)*	as required
vi.	Water	as required

Process:
i. The moyan is added in the flour.
ii. The finely minced fenugreek leaves and salt are mixed in the wheat flour.
iii. Water is added in the flour and it is kneaded to make dough.
iv. The dough is divided in to small Lois / Balls.
v. The Lois are rolled in to pancakes.
vi. The pancakes are deep fried in heated Ghee.

3. PAALAK BHAAJI POORIE (POORIE WITH SPINACH)

All the ingredients and the process remain same as above (Methi Poorie) except that spinach leaves are used in place of fenugreek leaves.

F. BHATHURAA

1. SAADAA BHATURAA (PLAIN BHATHURAA)

Ingredients:
i.	Maida flour	2 Cups
ii.	Water	as required
iii.	Ghee	as required

Optional ingredient:
Oil or Vanaspati could be used in place of Ghee.

Process:
i. The Moyan is mixed in the flour, and then it is kneaded with water to make dough.
ii. The dough is divided in to small Lois / Balls.
iii. The Lois are rolled in to pancakes.
iv. The pancakes are deep fried in the heated Ghee in a deep fry pan.

2. AJWAIN BHATHURAA (LOVAGE POORIE OF REFINED WHEAT FLOUR)

Maida is used in place of wheat flour in the recipe of Ajwain Paraathaa under the subject heading 'Paraathaa'.

3. MASAALAA BHATHURAA (SPICED POORIE OF REFINED WHEAT FLOUR)

Maida is used in place of wheat flour in the recipe of Masala Paraathaa under the subject heading 'Paraathaa'.

CHAPTER 4: RICE DISHES

1. BHAAT (WHITE RICE COOKED CLASSICALLY)

Generally the rice is cooked by adding the requisite quantity of water to rice and cooking in the pressure cooker or rice cooker. The process followed in Bundelkhand is the classical process, prescribed in the Ayurveda.

Process:
i. The rice is taken in the cooking Tabeli (A vessel with specific ratio of height and width).
ii. The water, as required for cooking in the pressure cooker or rice cooker, is added.
iii. Additional water, about 33% of above quantity, is added to it.
iv. The vessel is covered is placed on stove.
v. Once the steam starts coming out, the cover is slided slightly.
vi. When rice is partially cooked, the vessel is taken out and the extra water is drained off. This water is called 'Adan' and given to children for drinking as it is high in energy due to carbohydrate.
vii. The cooking process is continues to get perfectly cooked and separated rice grains.

The Bhaat is ready and is best served with hot Tuar Daal, garnished with Ghee or 'Baghaari Daal' (Fried Daal).

2. PEERO BHAAT (YELLOW RICE)

* Sufficient for 2 persons.

Generally the left-over cooked rice of the earlier day is used for this dish. Thus the stale dish is rendered tasty and consumed, avoiding the waste.

Ingredients:
i.	Left-over cooked white rice of earlier day	4 Cups
ii.	Turmeric powder	¼ Ts
iii.	Mustard (Big) seeds	¼ Ts

iv.	Black pepper (Ground)	¼ Ts
v.	Ghee	1 Tbs

Optional ingredients:
Ghee could be substituted with Vanaspati or oil.

Process:
i. The lumps of the stale rice are broken so that rice grains appear un-clustered.
ii. The Ghee is heated in the Deep frying pan.
iii. Mustard (Big) seeds and Black pepper are added and stirred.
iv. Turmeric powder is added and stirred to make homogeneous mixture with Ghee.
v. The rice from the Step # i is added in the Deep frying pan and mixed with continuous stirring till the rice becomes hot as well as uniformly yellow in color.

It is best served with Tomato Chatni or Lemon pickle.

3. MEETHI KHICHREE (SWEETENED RICE AND LENTIL COOKED DISH)

* **Sufficient for 2 persons.**

Ingredients:
i.	Rice	1 Cup
ii.	Pigeon pea	1 Cup
iii.	Jaggery	½ Cup
iv.	Water	as required
v.	Ghee	as required

Optional ingredient:
i. Green gram (Moong Daal) could be used in place of Pigeon pea (Tuar Daal).
ii. The proportion of rice and Daal (Lentil) is 50% each. This ratio could be changed to 60:40 or 40:60.
iii. Sugar could be used in place of Jaggery.

Process:

i. The rice and pigeon pea are washed, mixed and cooked together in the pressure cooker. The cooked product is called Khichri.
ii. The grated Jaggery is added in the Khichri and mixed well.

The Meethi Khichri is ready and should be served, garnished with Ghee. The Paapad and pickle are best accomplices.

4. NAMKEEN KHICHRI (SALTY KHICHRI)

* **Sufficient for 2 persons.**

Ingredients:

i.	Rice	1 Cup
ii.	Pigeon pea	1 Cup
iii.	Jaggery	½ Cup
iv.	Turmeric	¼ Ts
v.	Ginger	1 Ts
vi.	Garlic	1 Ts
vii.	Green chili	2 Ts
viii.	Water	as required
ix.	Salt	as required
x.	Ghee	2 Tbs

Optional ingredient:
i. Green gram (Moong Daal) could be used in place of Pigeon pea (Tuar Daal).
ii. The proportion of rice and Daal (Lentil) is 50% each. This ratio could be changed to 60:40 or 40:60.

Process:
i. The rice and pigeon pea are washed, mixed and cooked together in the pressure cooker. The cooked product is called Khichri.
ii. Ghee is heated in Deep frying pan and Turmeric powder, grated Ginger, Garlic, minced Green chili and salt are added and fried one by one and mixed.
iii. The Khichri is added to Deep frying pan and mixed well.

The Namkeen Khichri is ready and should be served, garnished with Ghee. The Paapad and pickle are best accomplices.

CHAPTER 5: SABJIYAA (VEGETABLE PREPARATIONS)

CURRIES: ACCOMPANIMENT TO ROTI AND RICE DISHES

In Bundelkhand, the spices are added minimally in order to protect and accentuate the original taste of the vegetable, legumes, Bari or daals. The enhancement of the taste is also achieved by varying the cooking process like roasting and boiling etc.

The desi (as against hybrid) tomatoes are used in Bundelkhand which have thin film like skin and high content of melic acid (hence they are sourer). So in order to retain the original taste of vegetables legumes, Bari or daals, the tomatoes are added in minimum quantity or avoided altogether.

A. RASILI SABJIYAA

KAND-MOOL KI RASILI SABJIYAA (ROOTS/ RHIZOMES/ TUBER/ ROOTS)

1. AALOO KI RASILI SABJI (POTATO CURRY)

Ingredient:
i.	Potatoes	250 Gm
ii.	Oil	2 Tbs
iii.	Onion	3 Tbs
iv.	Garlic	1 Ts
v.	Ginger	1 Ts
vi.	Green chilies	1 Tbs or to taste
vii.	Turmeric powder	½ Ts
viii.	Coriander seeds powder	1 Tbs
ix.	Cumin seeds	1 Ts

x.	Mustard seeds	¼ Ts
xi.	Red chili powder	1 Ts or to taste
xii.	Salt	to taste
xiii.	Kothambir	1 Tbs
xiv.	Water	as required

Process:
i. Ingredients # iii to vi are grated.
ii. Oil is heated in the frying pan on medium flame.
iii. Ingredients # iii to xi are added one by one and fried with continuous sautéing.
iv. The potatoes are cut in to small pieces (about 2 cm cubes) and added in the frying pan with continuous sautéing.
v. The water is added and the mix is sautéed.
vi. Salt is added and the mix is brought to a boil.
vii. The flame is reduced to low and the lid is covered on the fry pan. viii. Let it cook for 8-10 minutes or till the potatoes become tender / soft.
viii. Adjust the water to get the desired consistency.

The curry is transferred to the storage bowl, the minced Kothambir is added and mixed.
This curry could be served with both Roti and rice preparations.

There are two variations in the processing of potatoes;

A. The potatoes cooking process: In this process, the potatoes are cut in small pieces and added in the frying pan

B. The potatoes boiling process: In this process, the potatoes are boiled and cut in small pieces before adding in the frying pan. This process imparts thicker gravy due to part of potatoes disperse finely in the gravy. The taste is also superior.

2. RASILE ALOO TAMAATAR (POTATO WITH TOMATO CURRY)

This dish is prepared just like above 'Potato curry' except that 125 Gm Tomatoes are added at step # vi (After the mix has been brought to boil).

There are four variations in the processing of potatoes;

A. The potatoes cooking process: In this process, the potatoes are cut in small pieces and added in the frying pan

A-1: In this process, the Tomatoes are cut in small pieces and added.

A-2: In this process, the whole Tomatoes are boiled in water, then peeled and the pulp is mashed. This pulp is added.
This process imparts thicker gravy due to part of potatoes disperse finely in the gravy. The taste is superior.

B. The potatoes boiling process: In this process, the potatoes are boiled and cut in small pieces before adding in the frying pan. This process imparts thicker gravy due to part of potatoes disperse finely in the gravy. The taste is also superior.

B-1: In this process, the Tomatoes are cut in small pieces and added.

B-2: In this process, the whole Tomatoes are boiled in water, then peeled and the pulp is mashed. This pulp is added. This process imparts thicker gravy due to part of potatoes disperse finely in the gravy. The taste is far superior.

3. RASILE ALOO TAAJE MATAR TAMAATAR (PEAS, POTATO WITH TOMATO CURRY)

This dish is prepared just like above 'Potato Tomato Curry' except that 100 Gm Green Peas (Taaje Matar) are added at step # iv (After the addition of potatoes).

4. MOOLI KI RASILI SABJI (RADISH CURRY)

Ingredient:
i.	Radish	250 Gm
ii.	Oil	2 Tbs
iii.	Onion	3 Tbs
iv.	Green chilies	1 Tbs or to taste
v.	Turmeric powder	½ Ts
vi.	Coriander seeds powder	1 Tbs

vii.	Cumin seeds	1 Ts
viii.	Mustard seeds	¼ Ts
ix.	Red chili powder	1 Ts or to taste
x.	Salt	to taste
xi.	Kothambir	1 Tbs
xii.	Tomatos	100 Gms
xiii.	Water	as required

Process:
  i. Ingredients # iii and iv are grated.
  ii. Oil is heated in the frying pan on medium flame.
  iii. Ingredients # iii to ix are added one by one and fried with continuous sautéing.
  iv. The radishes are cut in to small pieces (about 1-1.5 cm cubes or in 1 cm thick round circles) and added in the frying pan with continuous sautéing. Tomatoes are grated and added to it and mix is cooked for five minutes.
  v. The water is added and the mix is sautéed.
  vi. Add the salt and bring the mix to a boil. Add the Tomatoes (Grated or cut in to pieces or boiled and mashed).
  vii. Reduce the flame to low and cover the lid on the fry pan. Let it cook for 8-10 minutes or the radish pieces become tender / soft.
  viii. Adjust the water to get the desired consistency.

The curry is transferred to the storage bowl; the minced Kothambir is added and mixed.

This curry could be served with both Roti and rice preparations.

5. *GHUYYAAN KI RASILI SABJI (COLOCASIA CURRY)*

Ingredient:
i.	Colocasia*	250 Gms
ii.	Oil	2 Tbs
iii.	Onion	3 Tbs
iv.	Green chilies	1 Tbs or to taste
v.	Turmeric powder	½ Ts
vi.	Coriander seeds powder	1 Tbs

vii.	Mustard seeds	¼ Ts
viii.	Lovage (Ajwain)	¼ Ts
ix.	Salt	to taste
x.	Tomatoes	100 Gms
xi.	Water	as required

Optional ingredients: Amchur 2 Ts (Raw mango powder) could be used in place of Tomatos.

Process:
i. Ingredients # iii and iv are grated.
ii. Oil is heated in the frying pan on medium flame.
iii. Ingredients # iii to viii are added one by one and fried with continuous sautéing.
iv. [*] The colocasia are peeled and cut in to small pieces (about 2 cm cubes) and added in the frying pan with continuous sautéing.
v. Add the Tomatoes (Grated or cut in to pieces or boiled and mashed)
vi. The water is added and the mix is sautéed. Grated Tomatoes are also added.
vii. Add the salt, bring the mix to a boil, and reduce the flame to low and cover the lid on the fry pan. Let it cook for 8-10 minutes or the potatoes become tender / soft.
viii. Adjust the water to get the desired consistency.

The curry is transferred to the storage bowl; the minced Kothambir is added and mixed.

This curry could be served with both Roti and rice preparations.

* Optional process: Colacasia could be boiled in water, then peeled and cut in to small pieces. This process imparts thicker gravy due to part of colacasia disperse finely in the gravy. The taste is also superior.

6. MURAAR KI RASILI SABJI (LOTUS STEMS CURRY)

The lotus stem should be cleaned thoroughly. Then its top layer is peeled off. The so cleaned stems are cut in to small pieces.

Ingredients:

i.	Lotus stem pieces	100 Gm
ii.	Water	as required
iii.	Oil	as required
iv.	Onion*	2 Tbs
v.	Garlic*	½ Ts
vi.	Ginger*	1 Ts
vii.	Turmeric	½ Ts
viii.	Mustard seeds	¼ Ts
ix.	Green chili*	1 Tbs
x.	Fenugreek seeds	¼ Ts
xi.	Salt	to taste
xii.	Special Garam Masala	½ Ts
xiii.	Tomatoes* (Grated paste)	2 Tbs
xiv.	Water	as required

Grated

Process:
i. The oil is heated in the deep frying pan and all the spices are added (step iv to x) and fried.
ii. The diced small pieces of the lotus stem are boiled in water to soften and then added in the oil and mixed. Grated Tomatoes are also added with sautéing.
iii. Salt is added and mixed. Special Garam masala is added and mixed.
iv. Sufficient water is added to form gravy. The lid is covered.
v. It is cooked uniformly for few minutes.

The Muraar ki Rasili Sabji is ready. This is served with Roti preparations.

II. SABJI-PHALON KI RASILI SABJI (CURRY OF FRUIT VEGETABLES)

1. TAMAATAR KI RASILI SABJI (TOMATO CURRY)

Ingredient:
i.	Tomatoes	250 Gm
ii.	Oil	2 Tbs
iii.	Onion	3 Tbs
iv.	Green chilies	1 Tbs or to taste
v.	Turmeric powder	½ Ts
vi.	Cumin seeds	1 Ts
vii.	Mustard seeds	¼ Ts
viii.	Fenugreek seeds	¼ Ts
ix.	Salt	to taste
x.	Sugar	2 Ts or to taste
xi.	Kothambir	1 Tbs
xii.	Water	as required

Optional ingredients: The grated ginger, garlic and the coriander powder could be added.

Process:
   i. Ingredients # iii and iv are grated.
   ii. Oil is heated in the frying pan on medium flame.
   iii. Ingredients # iii to viii are added one by one and fried with continuous sautéing.
   iv. The tomatoes are cut in to small pieces (about 2 cm cubes) and added in the frying pan with continuous sautéing.
   v. The water is added and the mix is sautéed.
   vi. Salt and sugar are added and mixed.
   vii. The flame is reduced to low and the lid is covered on the fry pan.
   viii. Let it cook for 8-10 minutes or till the mix becomes homogenous.
   ix. Adjust the water to get the desired consistency.

The curry is transferred to the storage bowl and the minced Kothambir is added with stirring. This curry could be served with both Roti and rice preparations.

Optional processes:
There are three variations in the processing of tomatoes;
1A: In this process, the Tomatoes are cut in small pieces and added.

1B: In this process, the Tomatoes are grated and the resultant paste is added.

1C. In this process, the whole Tomatoes are boiled in water, then peeled and the pulp is mashed. This pulp is added.

This process imparts thicker gravy due to part of potatoes disperse finely in the gravy. The taste is far superior.

2. LAUKI KI RASILI SABJI (ASH GOURD CURRY)

Ingredient:

#	Ingredient	Quantity
1.	Ash gourd	250 Gm
2.	Oil	2 Tbs
3.	Onion	3 Tbs
4.	Green chilies	1 Tbs or to taste
5.	Turmeric powder	½ Ts
6.	Cumin seeds	1½ Ts
7.	Mustard seeds	¼ Ts
8.	Tomatoes (Grated to paste)	½ Cup
9.	Salt	To taste
10.	Kothambir	1 Tbs
11.	Water	As Required

Process:
i. Ingredients # iii and iv are grated.
ii. Oil is heated in the frying pan on medium flame.
iii. Ingredients # iii to vii are added one by one and fried with continuous sautéing.
iv. The ash gourd is cut in to small pieces (about 2 cm cubes) and added in the frying pan with continuous sautéing.
v. The water is added and the mix is sautéed.
vi. The grated tomatoes are added. Salt is also added and mixed.
vii. The flame is reduced to low and the lid is covered on the fry pan.
viii. Let it cook for 8-10 minutes or till the mix becomes homogenous.
ix. Adjust the water to get the desired consistency.

The curry is transferred to the storage bowl and the minced Kothambir is added with stirring.

This curry could be served with both Roti and rice preparations.

3. PHADKULI KI RASILI SABJI (SMOOTH GOURD CURRY)

The ingredients and the process is as above (Lauki ki Rasili Sabji) except that ash gourd is replaced by smooth gourd.

4. RASILE BHATAA (BRINJAL CURRY)
Ingredient:
i.	Brinjal	250 Gm
	(Big size, minimum seeds)	
ii.	Oil	3 Tbs
iii.	Onion	4 Tbs
iv.	Green chilies	1 Tbs or to taste
v.	Coriander powder	2 Ts
vi.	Turmeric powder	½ Ts
vii.	Cumin seeds	1½ Ts
viii.	Mustard seeds	¼ Ts
ix.	Fenugreek seeds	¼ Ts
x.	Asafoetida	¼ Ts
xi.	Salt	to taste
xii.	Kothambir	1 Tbs
xiii.	Water	as required

Optional ingredients: The grated ginger, garlic and the coriander powder could be added. Tomatoes (½ Cup-grated) could be added.

Process:
  i. Ingredients # iii and iv are grated.
  ii. Oil is heated in the frying pan on medium flame.
  iii. Ingredients # iii to xi are added one by one and fried with continuous sautéing.

iv. The brinjals are cut in to small pieces (about 3-4 cm cube) and placed in a bowl of water. They are added in the frying pan with continuous sautéing.
v. The water is added and the mix is sautéed.
vi. The salt is also added and mixed.
vii. The flame is reduced to low and the lid is covered on the fry pan.
viii. Let it cook for 8-10 minutes or till the mix becomes homogenous.
ix. Adjust the water to get the desired consistency.

The curry is transferred to the storage bowl and the minced Kothambir is added with stirring.

This curry could be served with both Roti and rice preparations.

5. *PHOOL-GOBHI KI RASILI SABJI (CAULIFLOWER CURRY)*

Ingredient:
i.	Cauliflower	250 Gm
ii.	Oil	2 Tbs
iii.	Onion	3 Tbs
iv.	Ginger	2 Ts
v.	Garlic	2 Ts
vi.	Green chilies	1 Tbs or to taste
vii.	Coriander powder	2 Ts
viii.	Turmeric powder	½ Ts
ix.	Cumin seeds	1½ Ts
x.	Mustard seeds	¼ Ts
xi.	Fenugreek seeds	¼ Ts
xii.	Tomatoes (Grated to paste)	½ Cup
xiii.	Salt	to taste
xiv.	Kothambir	1 Tbs
xv.	Water	as required

Process:
i. Ingredients # iii to vi are grated.
ii. Oil is heated in the frying pan on medium flame.

- iii. Ingredients # iii to xi are added one by one and fried with continuous sautéing.
- iv. The cauliflower is cut in to small pieces (about 2 cm size individual flower bunch) and added in the frying pan with continuous sautéing.
- v. The water is added and the mix is sautéed.
- vi. The grated tomatoes are added.
- vii. Salt is also added and mixed.
- viii. The flame is reduced to low and the lid is covered on the fry pan.
- ix. Let it cook for 8-10 minutes or till the mix becomes homogenous.
- x. Adjust the water to get the desired consistency.

The curry is transferred to the storage bowl and the minced Kothambir is added with stirring.

This curry could be served with both Roti and rice preparations.

6. PATTAA-GOBHI KI RASILI SABJI (CABBAGE CURRY):

The ingredients and the process is as above (Phool Gobi ki Rasili Sabji) except that cauliflower is replaced by cabbage.

7. TAAJE MATAR KI RASILI SABJI (GREEN PEAS CURRY):

Ingredient:
- i. Green peas*   100 Gm
- ii. Oil   2 Tbs
- iii. Onion   3 Tbs
- iv. Ginger   2 Ts
- v. Garlic   2 Ts
- vi. Green chilies   1 Tbs or to taste
- vii. Coriander powder   2 Ts
- viii. Turmeric powder   ½ Ts

ix.	Cumin seeds	1½ Ts
x.	Mustard seeds	¼ Ts
xi.	Fenugreek seeds	¼ Ts
xii.	Tomatoes *(Grated to paste)*	½ Cup
xiii.	Salt	to taste
xiv.	Asafoetida	equal to small size pea
xv.	Water	as required

* The green peas could be used as such or after crushing them lightly.

Process:
   i. Ingredients # iii to vi are grated.
   ii. Oil is heated in the frying pan on medium flame.
   iii. Ingredients # iii to xi are added one by one and fried with continuous sautéing.
   iv. The green peas are added in the frying pan with continuous sautéing.
   v. The water is added and the mix is sautéed.
   vi. The grated tomatoes are added.
   vii. Salt is also added and mixed.
   viii. The flame is reduced to low and the lid is covered on the fry pan.
   ix. Let it cook for 8-10 minutes or till the mix becomes homogenous.
   x. Adjust the water to get the desired consistency.
   xi. The curry is transferred to the storage bowl and the minced
   xii. Kothambir is added with stirring.

The Baghaar: The oil is heated in an earthen Diyaa, held by a tong or stainless steel spoon. The Ghee and asafetida are placed in it. The Diyaa is heated, on the direct flame, till it become red hot and smoking. Then this Diyaa is dipped in the curry and the lid is covered. One should be careful as the flames and smoke come out rapidly when the red hot Diyaa / Stainless Steel spoon (and the smoking spices in it) touches the Daal.

This curry could be served with both Roti and rice preparations.

8. KACHCHE CHANE / CHANAA BOOT KI RASILI SABJI (GREEN / RAW CHICKPEA CURRY):

The ingredients and the process is as above (Taaje Matar ki Rasili Sabji) except that Matar is replaced by Kachchaa Chanaa.

The Kachche Chane could be used as such or after crushing them lightly.

9. KACHCHE GULAABI CHANE KI RASILI SABJI (GREEN CHHOLE CHICKPEA CURRY):

The ingredients and the process is as above (Taaje Matar ki Rasili Sabji) except that Matar is replaced by Kachchaa Gulaabi Chanaa.

The Kachche Gulaabi Chane could be used as such or after crushing them lightly.

10. PARVAL KI RASILI SABJI (TRICHOSANTHES DIOICA CURRY):

Ingredient:

i.	Parval	250 Gm
ii.	Oil	2 Tbs
iii.	Onion	3 Tbs
iv.	Green chilies	1 Tbs or to taste
v.	Coriander powder	2 Ts
vi.	Turmeric powder	½ Ts
vii.	Cumin seeds	1½ Ts
viii.	Mustard seeds	¼ Ts
ix.	Tomatoes (Grated to paste)	½ Cup
x.	Salt	to taste
xi.	Kothambir	1 Tbs
xii.	Water	as required

Optional ingredients: The grated ginger, garlic and the coriander powder could be added.

Process:
i. Ingredients # iii to vi are grated.
ii. Oil is heated in the frying pan on medium flame.
iii. Ingredients # iii and iv are added one by one and fried with continuous sautéing.
iv. The Parval fruits are cut in to small pieces (about 1 cm size circles) and added in the frying pan with continuous sautéing. The water is added and the mix is sautéed.
v. The grated tomatoes are added.
vi. Salt is also added and mixed.
vii. The flame is reduced to low and the lid is covered on the fry pan.
viii. Let it cook for 10-12 minutes or till the Parval pieces become soft / tender.
ix. Adjust the water to get the desired consistency.
x. The curry is transferred to the storage bowl and the minced Kothambir is added with stirring.

This curry could be served with both Roti and rice preparations.

11. KUNDROO KI RASILI SABJI (GHERKINS):

The ingredients and the process is as above (Parval ki Rasili Sabji) except that Parval is replaced by Kundroo.

12. KONS (MUNGAA) KI RASILI SABJI (DRUMSTICK CURRY):

Ingredient:
i. Drumsticks   12 pieces (2-2.5" Long)
ii. Oil   2 Tbs
iii. Onion   3 Tbs
iv. Green chilies   1 Tbs or to taste
v. Coriander powder   2 Ts
vi. Turmeric powder   ½ Ts

vii.	Cumin seeds	1½ Ts
viii.	Mustard seeds	¼ Ts
ix.	Tomatoes *(Grated to paste)*	½ Cup
x.	Salt	to taste
xi.	Special Garam Masala	1 Ts
xii.	Kothambir	1 Tbs
xiii.	Water	as required

Optional ingredients:
The potatoes (1 Cup 2 cm cube size small pieces) could be added. The grated ginger and garlic could be added.

Process:
i. Ingredients # iii and iv are grated.
ii. Oil is heated in the frying pan on medium flame.
iii. Ingredients # iii and iv are added one by one and fried with continuous sautéing.
iv. The Drumsticks are cut in to small pieces (about 2 to 2.5" long) and added in the frying pan with continuous sautéing.
v. The water is added and the mix is sautéed.
vi. The grated tomatoes are added.
vii. Salt is also added and mixed.
viii. The flame is reduced to low and the lid is covered on the fry pan.
ix. Let it cook for 15-20 minutes or till the drumsticks become soft / tender.
x. Adjust the water to get the desired consistency.
xi. The Special Garam Masala is added with mixing.
xii. The curry is transferred to the storage bowl and the minced Kothambir is added with stirring.

This curry could be served with both Roti and rice preparations.

13. KUMHARAA KI RASILI SABJI (PUMPKIN CURRY):

Ingredient:
i.	Pumpkin	250 Gm
ii.	Oil	1 Tbs
iii.	Onion	3 Tbs

iv.	Green chilies	1 Tbs or to taste
v.	Turmeric powder	½ Ts
vi.	Cumin seeds	1 Ts
vii.	Mustard seeds	¼ Ts
viii.	Salt	to taste
ix.	Sugar	2 Ts or to taste
x.	Water	as required

Optional ingredients: The grated ginger, garlic and the coriander powder could be added.

Process:
i. Ingredients # iii and iv are grated.
ii. Oil is heated in the frying pan on medium flame.
iii. Ingredients # iii to vii are added one by one and fried with continuous sautéing.
iv. The Pumpkin is peeled and cut in to small pieces (about 2 cm cubes) and added in the frying pan with continuous sautéing.
v. The water is added and the mix is sautéed.
vi. Salt and sugar are added and mixed.
vii. The flame is reduced to low and the lid is covered on the fry pan.
viii. Let it cook for 8-10 minutes or till the mix becomes homogenous.
ix. Adjust the water to get the desired consistency.
x. The curry is transferred to the storage bowl and the minced Kothambir is added with stirring.

This curry could be served with both Roti and rice preparations.

III. KACHCHE PHALON KI RASILI SABJI (RAW FRUITS)

1. KACHCHE PAPITAA KI RASILI SABJI (RAW PAPAYA CURRY):

Ingredient:
i.	Raw papaya	100 Gm
ii.	Oil	2 Tbs

iii.	Onion	3 Tbs
iv.	Ginger	2 Ts
v.	Garlic	2 Ts
vi.	Green chilies	1 Tbs or to taste
vii.	Coriander powder	2 Ts
viii.	Turmeric powder	½ Ts
ix.	Cumin seeds	1½ Ts
x.	Mustard seeds	¼ Ts
xi.	Tomatoes *(Grated to paste)*	½ Cup
xii.	Salt	to taste
xiii.	xiii. Water	as required

Process:
   i. Ingredients # iii to vi are grated.
   ii. Oil is heated in the frying pan on medium flame.
   iii. Ingredients # iii to x are added one by one and fried with continuous sautéing.
   iv. The raw papaya is cut in to 2cm size cube like pieces and are added in the frying pan with continuous sautéing.
   v. The water is added and the mix is sautéed.
   vi. The grated tomatoes are added.
   vii. Salt is also added and mixed.
   viii. The flame is reduced to low and the lid is covered on the fry pan.
   ix. Let it cook for 10-12 minutes or till the mix becomes homogenous.
   x. Adjust the water to get the desired consistency.
   xi. The curry is transferred to the storage bowl and the minced Kothambir is added with stirring.

This curry could be served with both Roti and rice preparations.

IV. SOOKHE BEEJO KI RASILI SABJIYAA (DRIED / PRESERVED LEGUMES' CURRY)

1. GULAABI CHANE / CHHOLE KI RASILI SABJI (CHHOLE CURRY):

Ingredient:

i.	Green peas*	250 Gm
ii.	Oil	4 Tbs
iii.	Onion	½ Cup
iv.	Ginger	1 Tbs
v.	Garlic	1 Tbs
vi.	Green chilies	2 Tbs or to taste
vii.	Coriander powder	1 Tbs
viii.	Turmeric powder	½ Ts
ix.	Cumin seeds	2 Ts
x.	Mustard seeds	¼ Ts
xi.	Fenugreek seeds	¼ Ts
xii.	Tomatoes (Grated to paste)	1½ Cup
xiii.	Salt	to taste
xiv.	Special Garam Masala	2 Ts
xv.	Water	as required

* The green peas could be used as such or after crushing them lightly.

Process:
  i. Ingredients # iii to vi are grated.
  ii. Oil is heated in the frying pan on medium flame.
  iii. Ingredients # iii to xi are added one by one and fried with continuous sautéing.
  iv. The water is added in the Chhole and they are cooked in the pressure cooker.
  v. These softened Chhole are added in the frying pan with continuous sautéing.
  vi. The water is added and the mix is sautéed.
  vii. The grated tomatoes are added.
  viii. Salt is also added and mixed.
  ix. The flame is reduced to low and the lid is covered on the fry pan.
  x. Crush some Chholes by flat spatula so that they become paste and improve the thickness of the gravy.
  xi. Let it cook for 10-15 minutes or till the mix becomes homogenous.
  xii. Adjust the water to get the desired consistency.
  The curry is transferred to the storage bowl and the minced

xiii.   Kothambir is added with stirring.
xiv.   This curry is served garnished with the onion pieces.

2. SOOKHI MATAR KI RASILI SABJI (DRY PEAS CURRY):

The ingredients and the process are as above (Chhole curry) except that dry peas replace the Chhole.

3. SOOKHE CHANE KI RASILI SABJI (BLACK CHANAA CURRY):

The ingredients and the process are as above (Chhole curry) except that black Chanaa replace the Chhole.

V. TEL-BEEJO KI RASILI SABJI (OILSEEDS CURRY)

1. TILI KI RASILI SABJI (SESAME SEEDS):

Actually the word 'Curry' is misnomer in this case as this is only the gravy but serves as curry.

Ingredient:
i.	Sesame seeds	100 Gm
ii.	Oil	2 Tbs
iii.	Onion	½ Cup
iv.	Green chilies	1 Tbs or to taste
v.	Turmeric powder	½ Ts
vi.	Cumin seeds	1 Ts
vii.	Salt	to taste
viii.	Water	as required

Optional ingredients: The grated ginger, garlic and the coriander powder could be added.

Process:

i. The sesame seeds are soaked in water overnight and grinded to a paste next day.
ii. Onion and green chilies are also grinded to a paste.
iii. Oil is heated in the frying pan on medium flame.
iv. Turmeric powder and cumin seeds are added in oil with sautéing.
v. The onion and green chili paste is added and fried with continuous sautéing.
vi. The sesame seeds paste is added and sautéed.
vii. Salt is added and mixed.
viii. The flame is reduced to low and the lid is covered on the fry pan.
ix. Let it cook for 8-10 minutes.
x. The curry is transferred to the storage bowl.
xi. This curry could be served with both Roti and rice preparations.

2. *MOONG-PHALLI KI RASILI SABJI (GROUNDNUT CURRY):*

The ingredients and the process are as above (Tili ki Rasili Sabji) except that groundnuts replace the Chhole.

B. SOOKHI SABJI (DRY VEGETABLE DISHES / WITHOUT GRAVY)

I. ROOTS/ RHIZOMES/ TUBER/ ROOTS

1. AALOO KI SOOKHI SABJI (POTATO DRY VEG)

Ingredients:
i. Potatoes   250 Gm
ii. Oil   3 Tbs
iii. Onion   ½ Cup
iv. Green chilies   1 Tbs or to taste

v.	Turmeric powder	½ Ts
vi.	Cumin seeds	1½ Ts
vii.	Salt	to taste
viii.	Kothambir	2 Tbs
ix.	Water	as required

Optional ingredients: The grated ginger, garlic and the coriander powder could be added.

Process:
i. The potatoes are peeled and cut in to small pieces (about 2 cm cubes like).
ii. Onion and green chilies are grated.
iii. Oil is heated in the frying pan on medium flame.
iv. Turmeric powder and cumin seeds are added in oil with sautéing.
v. The grated onion and green chilies are added and fried with continuous sautéing.
vi. The potato pieces are added and sautéed.
vii. Salt is added and mixed. Water is added.
viii. The flame is reduced to low and the lid is covered on the fry pan.
ix. Let it cook for 10-15 minutes or till the water gets evaporated.
x. The curry is transferred to the storage bowl.

This curry is garnished with minced Kothambir and served with both Roti and rice preparations.

Optional process: Potatoes could be boiled, peeled, cut in to small pieces and added in the fry pan.

2. SOOKHI MASALA GHUIYAA (DRY SPICED COLOCASIA VEG)

2A. SOOKHI MASALA GHUIYAA-I

* Sufficient for 2 persons.

Ingredients:
i.	Arbi (Colocasia)	250 Gm
ii.	Water	as required

iii.	Oil*	as required
iv.	Mustard seeds	¼ Ts
v.	Asafoetida	¼ Ts
vi.	Red chili powder	½ Ts
vii.	Turmeric powder	¼ Ts
viii.	Ajwain	¼ Ts
ix.	Salt	to taste
x.	Amchur (Powdered dried raw mango)	½ Ts
xi.	Special Garam Masala	½ Ts
xii.	Kothambir	1 Tbs

* Liberal quantity is required for frying Arbi.

Process:
i. The Arbi roots are steam-cooked in a pressure cooker (or otherwise) to soften them.
ii. They are peeled and sliced them in to smaller round pieces.
iii. The oil is heated in the Deep frying pan and mustard seeds are added.
iv. When they start crackling, the spices # v to viii are added and fried at low flame.
v. The Arabi pieces are added in the Deep frying pan with the continuous mixing. Add salt and cook till they turn golden.
vi. The Amchur powder and Special garam masala are added and mixed.
vii. Finally the mince Kothambir are added and mixed.

The Dry spiced Colocasia Veg is ready to be served.

2B. GHUYYAAN KI SOOKHI SABJI-II

Ingredients:
i.	Colocasia	250 Gm
ii.	Oil	3 Tbs
iii.	Onion	3 Tbs
iv.	Green chilies	1 Tbs or to taste
v.	Turmeric powder	½ Ts

vi.	Coriander seeds powder	1 Tbs
vii.	Mustard seeds	¼ Ts
viii.	Lovage (Ajwain)	¼ Ts
ix.	Salt	to taste
x.	Tomatoes	2 Ts
xi.	Water	as required

Process:
  i. Ingredients # iii and iv are grated.
  ii. Oil is heated in the frying pan on medium flame.
  iii. Ingredients # iii to viii are added one by one and fried with continuous sautéing.
  iv. Colacasia are boiled in water, then peeled and cut in to small pieces (about 2 cm cubes) and added in the frying pan with continuous sautéing.
  v. Add grated Tomatoes paste with sautéing.
  vi. Add the salt and reduce the flame to low and cover the lid on the fry pan.
  vii. Let it cook for 5-6 minutes.
  viii. The cooked veg is transferred to the storage bowl; the minced Kothambir is added and mixed.

3. MASALA SHAKLAA SOOKHAA (SPICED SWEET POTATO DRY VEG)

Ingredients:

i.	Sweet Potato tubers	250 Gm
ii.	Water	as required
iii.	Oil*	as required
iv.	Mustard seeds	¼ Ts
v.	Red chili powder	½ Ts
vi.	Turmeric powder	¼ Ts
vii.	Salt	to taste
viii.	Special Garam Masala	½ Ts
ix.	Kothambir	1 Tbs

* Liberal quantity is required for frying Arbi.

Process:
  i. The Shaklaa Tubers are steam cooked in a pressure cooker (or otherwise) to soften them.
  ii. They are peeled and sliced them in to smaller round pieces.
  iii. The oil is heated in the Deep frying pan and mustard seeds are added.
  iv. When they start crackling, the spices # v and vi are added and fried at low flame.
  v. The Sweet Potato pieces are added in the Deep frying pan with the continuous mixing. Add salt and cook till they turn golden.
  vi. The Special garam masala is added and mixed.
  vii. Finally the mince Kothambir are added and mixed.

The Dry spiced Sweet Potato is ready to be served.

4. MURAAR KI SOOKHI SABJI (LOTUS STEMS DRY VEG)

The lotus stem should be cleaned thoroughly. Then its top layer is peeled off.

The so cleaned stems are cut in to small pieces.

Ingredients:

i.	Lotus stem pieces	100 Gms
ii.	Water	as required
iii.	Oil	as required
iv.	Onion*	2 Tbs
v.	Garlic*	½ Ts
vi.	Ginger*	1 Ts
vii.	Turmeric	½ Ts
viii.	Mustard seeds	¼ Ts
ix.	Green chili*	1 Tbs
x.	Salt	

xi.	Special Garam masala	½ Ts
xii.	Tomatoes* Grated	2 Tbs

Process:

i. The oil is heated in the deep frying pan and all the spices are added (step iv to ix) and fried.

ii. The diced small pieces of the lotus stem are boiled in water to soften and then added in the oil and mixed. Grated tomatoes are mixed with sautéing.

iii. Salt is added and mixed. Special Garam masala is added and mixed.

iv. About 2 Tbs water is sprinkled on it and lid is covered.

v. It is cooked uniformly for few minutes.

The Muraar ki Sookhi Sabji is ready. This is served with Roti preparations.

5. KAMAL-GATTA KI SOOKHI SABJI (LOTUS FRUIT-SEEDS DRY SABJI)

The Kamal-gatta fruit is torn and the seeds are taken out. The greenish cover of the seeds is removed (It is very bitter). These white soft seeds are sweet in taste.

Ingredients:

i.	Lotus fruit seeds	50 Gm
ii.	Onion*	1 Tbs
iii.	Garlic*	½ Ts
iv.	Ginger*	½ Ts

v.	Turmeric	¼ Ts
vi.	Mustard seeds	25-30 seeds
vii.	Green chili*	2 Ts
viii.	Salt	as required
ix.	Special Garam masala	¼ Ts
x.	Oil	as required
xi.	Water	

* Grated

Optional ingredients:

Tomato could be added if desired so.

Process:

i. The oil is heated in the deep frying pan and all the spices are added (step ii to vii) and fried.
ii. The diced small pieces of the lotus fruit seeds are added to it and mixed. Salt is added and mixed. Special Garam masala is added and mixed.
iii. About 1Tbs water is sprinkled on it and lid is covered.
iv. It is cooked uniformly for few minutes.

The Kamal-gatta ki Sookhi Sabji is ready. This is served with Roti preparations.

6. SINGHAARE KI SOOKHI SABJI (WATER CHESTNUT DRY VEG)

Ingredients:

i.	Water chestnuts (Boiled, de-shelled and cut in small pieces)	250 Gm
ii.	Oil	3 Tbs
iii.	Onion	3 Tbs
iv.	Green chilies	1 Tbs or to taste

v.	Turmeric powder	½ Ts
vi.	Coriander seeds powder	1 Tbs
vii.	Lovage (Ajwain)	¼ Ts
viii.	Salt	to taste
ix.	Tomatoes	2 Tbs
x.	Water	as required

Process:
i. Ingredients # iii and iv are grated.
ii. Oil is heated in the frying pan on medium flame.
iii. Ingredients # iii to viii are added one by one and fried with continuous sautéing.
iv. Colacasia are boiled in water, then peeled and cut in to small pieces (about 2 cm cubes) and added in the frying pan with continuous sautéing.
v. Add grated tomatoes paste with sautéing.
vi. Add the salt and reduce the flame to low and cover the lid on the fry pan. Let it cook for 5-6 minutes.
vii. The cooked veg is transferred to the storage bowl.

7. SOORAN KI SOOKHI SABJI (YAM DRY VEG)

Ingredients:

i.	Sooran (Yam) *(Boiled, peeled and cut in small pieces)*	250 Gm
ii.	Oil	3 Tbs
iii.	Onion	3 Tbs
iv.	Green chilies	1 Tbs or to taste
v.	Turmeric powder	½ Ts
vi.	Coriander seeds powder	1 Tbs
vii.	Lovage (Ajwain)	¼ Ts
viii.	Salt	to taste
ix.	Tomatoes	2 Tbs
x.	Water	as required

Process:
i. Ingredients # iii and iv are grated.
ii. Oil is heated in the frying pan on medium flame.
iii. Ingredients # iii to viii are added one by one and fried with continuous sautéing.
iv. Yam is peeled, then boiled in water and cut in to small pieces (about 2 cm cubes) and added in the frying pan with continuous sautéing.
v. Add grated tomatoes paste with sautéing.
vi. Add the salt and reduce the flame to low and cover the lid on the fry pan. Let it cook for 5-6 minutes.
vii. The cooked veg is transferred to the storage bowl.

8. KISARUYAA SOOKHI SABJI (A LOCAL ROOT VEGETABLE)

Ingredients:

i.	Kisaruyaa (Peeled and cut in small pieces)	100 Gms
ii.	Oil	2 Tbs
iii.	Onion	2 Tbs
iv.	Green chilies	1 Tbs or to taste
v.	Turmeric powder	¼ Ts
vi.	Coriander seeds powder	2 Ts
vii.	Salt	to taste
viii.	Amchur	1 Ts
ix.	Water	as required

Process:
i. Ingredients # iii and iv are grated.
ii. Oil is heated in the frying pan on medium flame.
iii. Ingredients # iii to vii are added one by one and fried with continuous sautéing.
iv. Yam is peeled, then boiled in water and cut in to small pieces (about 2 cm cubes) and added in the frying pan with continuous sautéing.
v. Add Amchur with sautéing.
vi. Add the salt and reduce the flame to low and cover the lid on the fry pan.

vii. Let it cook for 10-12 minutes or till such time when Kisaruyaa become tender / soft.
viii. The cooked veg is transferred to the storage bowl.

9. MOOLI KI SOOKHI SABJI (RADISH DRY VEG)

Ingredients:

i.	Radish (Peeled and cut in small pieces)	100 Gm
ii.	Oil	as required
iii.	Onion*	2 Tbs
iv.	Garlic*	½ Ts
v.	Ginger*	1 Ts
vi.	Turmeric	½ Ts
vii.	Mustard seeds	¼ Ts
viii.	Green chili*	1 Tbs
ix.	Salt	to taste
x.	Special Garam Masala	½ Ts

* Grated

Optional ingredients: Tomato could be added if desired.

Process:

i. The oil is heated in the deep frying pan and all the spices are added (step iv to ix) and fried.
ii. The diced small pieces of the radish are added in the oil and mixed.
iii. Salt is added and mixed. Special Garam masala is added and mixed.
iv. About 2 Tbs water is sprinkled on it and lid is covered.
v. It is cooked uniformly for few minutes.
vi. The Mooli ki Sookhi Sabji is ready. This is served with Roti or Rice preparations.

10. GAAJAR KI SOOKHI SABJI (CARROT DRY VEG)

Ingredients:

i.	Carrot (Peeled and cut in small pieces)	250 Gm

ii.	Oil	3 Tbs
iii.	Onion	3 Tbs
iv.	Ginger	3 Tbs
v.	Red chili powder	1 Ts or to taste
vi.	Turmeric powder	½ Ts
vii.	Coriander seeds powder	1 Tbs
viii.	Salt	to taste
ix.	Water	as required

Process:
   i. Ingredients # iii and iv are grated.
   ii. Oil is heated in the frying pan on medium flame.
   iii. Ingredients # iii to vii are added one by one and fried with continuous sautéing.
   iv. Carrot is peeled, cut in to small pieces (about 2 cm cubes) and added in the frying pan with continuous sautéing.
   v. Add the salt and reduce the flame to low and cover the lid on the fry pan.
   vi. Let it cook for 10-12 minutes or till the time when carrot pieces become tender / soft.
   vii. The cooked veg is transferred to the storage bowl.

II. PHOOL KI SOOKHI SABJI (FLOWER VEG CURRYLESS)

1. KERAA KE PHOOL KI SABJI (BANANA FLOWER VEG CURRYLESS)

Ingredients:

i.	Banana flowers	250 Gm
ii.	Oil	2 Tbs
iii.	Onion	3 Tbs
iv.	Garlic	1 Ts
v.	Ginger	1 Ts
vi.	Green chilies	1 Tbs or to taste
vii.	Turmeric powder	½ Ts
viii.	Coriander seeds powder	1Tbs
ix.	Salt	to taste
x.	Kothambir	1 Tbs

| xi. | Water | as required |

Process:
i. Ingredients # iii to vi are grated.
ii. Oil is heated in the frying pan on medium flame.
iii. Ingredients # iii to ix are added one by one and fried with continuous sautéing.
iv. The tip and tail of Banana flowers is cut. They are chopped in two pieces each (Individual bud). Then they are added in the frying pan with continuous sautéing.
v. The water is added and the mix is sautéed.
vi. Add the salt, bring the mix to a boil, reduce the flame to low and cover the lid on the fry pan. Let it cook for 8-10 minutes.
vii. The curry is transferred to the storage bowl, the minced Kothambir is added and mixed.
viii. This dish should be served with Roti preparations.

2. SEMAR KE PHOOL KI SABJI (SILK COTTON FLOWERS VEG CURRYLESS)

Ingredients:
i.	Silk cotton flowers	100 Gm
ii.	Oil	2 Tbs
iii.	Onion	3 Tbs
iv.	Green chilies	1 Tbs or to taste
v.	Turmeric powder	½ Ts
vi.	Coriander seeds powder	1 Tbs
vii.	Salt	to taste
viii.	Amchur	1 Ts

Process:
i. Ingredients # iii and iv are grated.
ii. Oil is heated in the frying pan on medium flame.
iii. Ingredients # iii to vi are added one by one and fried with continuous sautéing.

iv. The petals of silk cotton flowers are separated. They are chopped in small pieces. Then they are added in the frying pan with continuous sautéing.
v. Reduce the flame to low and cover the lid on the fry pan. Let it cook for 5-6 minutes.
vi. The curry is transferred to the storage bowl.
vii. This dish should be served with Roti preparations.

III. PHALLIYO KI SOOKHI SABJI (BEANS DRY VEGETABLE)

1. GAVAAR PHALLI KI SOOKHI MASALEDAR SABJI: (CLUSTER BEANS SPICY DRY VEG)

Ingredients:
i.	Cluster beans	250 Gm
ii.	Oil	2 Tbs
iii.	Garlic	1 Tbs
iv.	Green chilies	1 Tbs or to taste
v.	Turmeric powder	½ Ts
vi.	Cumin seeds	1½ Ts
vii.	Mustard seeds	¼ Ts
viii.	Tomatoes (Grated to paste)	½ Cup
ix.	Special Garam Masala	1 Ts
x.	Salt	to taste
xi.	Water	as required

Process:
i. Ingredients # iii and iv are grated.
ii. Oil is heated in the frying pan on medium flame.
iii. Ingredients # iii to vii are added one by one and fried with continuous sautéing.
iv. The both ends of cluster beans are cut and removed. Then the beans are cut in to 1-2 cm long pieces.
v. These pieces are added in the frying pan with continuous sautéing.
vi. The grated tomatoes are added.
vii. Salt is also added and mixed. Special Garam Masala is added with sautéing.
viii. The flame is reduced to low, the lid is covered on the fry pan.

ix. Let it cook for 8-10 minutes or till the beans are cooked and water is mostly evaporated.
x. The Cluster Beans Dry Veg is transferred to the storage bowl.

2. SEM PHALLI KI SOOKHI MASAALEDAAR SABJI (FLAT BEANS SPICY DRY VEG)

The ingredients and the process is as above (Cluster Beans Dry Veg) except that Sem phalli replace the Cluster beans.

3. FANSI PHALLI KI SOOKHI MASAALEDAAR SABJI (FRENCH BEANS SPICY DRY VEG)

The ingredients and the process is as above (Cluster Beans Dry Veg) except that French beans replace the Cluster beans.

IV. KACHCHE PHALON KI SOOKHI SABJIYAA (GRAVYLESS VEGETABLES OF RAW FRUITS)

1. ADH-PAKI BIHI KI SABJI (SEMI RIPE GUAVA VEG GRAVYLESS)

Ingredients:
i.	Guava (Semi ripe)	250 Gm
ii.	Oil	2 Tbs
iii.	Green chilies	1 Tbs or to taste
iv.	Turmeric powder	½ Ts
v.	Cumin seeds (whole)	1 Ts
vi.	Cumin seeds (powder)	1 Ts
vii.	Black Salt	½ Ts or to taste
viii.	Rock salt	½ Ts or to taste
ix.	Salt	to taste

Process:
i. Green chilies are minced.
ii. Oil is heated in the frying pan on medium flame.
iii. Ingredients # iii to vi are added one by one and fried with continuous sautéing.

iv. The both ends of guavas are cut and removed. Then the guavas are washed thoroughly and then grated.
v. This grate is added in the frying pan with continuous sautéing.
vi. Salt is also added and mixed. The rock salt and the black salt are added with sautéing.
vii. The flame is reduced to low, the lid is covered on the fry pan.
viii. Let it cook for 8-10 minutes.
ix. The Guava Dry Veg is transferred to the storage bowl.

2. KACHCHO PAPITAA (RAW PAPAYA VEG GRAVYLESS)

Ingredients:
i.	Raw papaya	250 Gm
ii.	Oil	2 Tbs
iii.	Onion	½ Cup
iv.	Ginger	2 Ts
v.	Green chilies	1 Tbs or to taste
vi.	Turmeric powder	½ Ts
vii.	Cumin seeds	1 Ts
viii.	Tomatoes	½ Cup
ix.	Salt	to taste
x.	Water	as required

Process:
i. Onion, ginger and Green chilies are grated.
ii. Oil is heated in the frying pan on medium flame.
iii. Ingredients # iii to viii are added one by one and fried with continuous sautéing.
iv. The both ends of papaya are cut and discarded. Then the papaya is washed thoroughly. If possible, peeling is avoided. It is cut into 1-2 cm cube like pieces.
v. These pieces are added in the frying pan with continuous sautéing.
vi. Salt is also added and mixed. The tomatoes are grated and added with sautéing.
vii. The flame is reduced to low, the lid is covered on the fry pan.
viii. Cook for 8-10 minutes or till the papaya pieces are softened.
ix. The Raw Papaya Dry Veg is transferred to the storage bowl.

3. KACHCHE KERAA KI SOOKHI SABJI (RAW BANANA VEG GRAVYLESS)

Ingredients:

i.	Raw Bananas	250 Gm
ii.	Oil	2 Tbs
iii.	Onion	½ Cup
iv.	Ginger	2 Ts
v.	Green chilies	1 Tbs or to taste
vi.	Turmeric powder	½ Ts
vii.	Cumin seeds	1 Ts
viii.	Lemon juice	1 Ts
ix.	Salt	to taste
x.	Water	as required

Process:
i. Onion, ginger and Green chilies are grated.
ii. Oil is heated in the frying pan on medium flame.
iii. Ingredients # iii to viii are added one by one and fried with continuous sautéing.
iv. The both ends of banana are cut and discarded. Then the banana is lightly peeled.
v. Papaya is cut into 1 cm thick rounds.
vi. These pieces are added in the frying pan with continuous sautéing.
vii. Salt is also added and mixed. The required amount of water is added. The lemon juice is added.
viii. The flame is reduced to low, the lid is covered on the fry pan.
ix. Let it cook for 8-10 minutes or till the banana pieces are cooked / softened and excess water is evaporated.
x. The Raw Banana Dry Veg is transferred to the storage bowl.

V. SOOKHE BEEJON KI SOOKHI SABJI (DRIED / PRESERVED VEGETABLES)

Common optional ingredient: Sodium bi carbonate could be added in water during initial cooking of beans for their faster softening.

1. SOOKHE GULAABI CHANE / CHHOLE KI SABJI (CHHOLE DRY VEG)

Ingredients:

i.	Dry Chhole	250 Gm
ii.	Oil	4 Tbs
iii.	Onion	1 Cup
iv.	Ginger	1 Tbs
v.	Garlic	1 Tbs
vi.	Green chilies	2 Tbs or to taste
vii.	Coriander powder	1 Tbs
viii.	Turmeric powder	½ Ts
ix.	Cumin seeds	2 Ts
x.	Mustard seeds	¼ Ts
xi.	Fenugreek seeds	¼ Ts
xii.	Tomatoes (Grated to paste)	½ Cup
xiii.	Salt	to taste
xiv.	Special Garam Masala	2 Ts
xv.	Kothambir	2 Tbs
xvi.	Water	as required

Optional ingredients: Red chili powder and Black salt could added.

Process:
i. Ingredients # iii to vi are grated.
ii. Oil is heated in the frying pan on medium flame.
iii. Ingredients # iii to xi are added one by one and fried with continuous sautéing.
iv. The water is added in the Chhole and they are cooked in the pressure cooker.
v. These softened Chhole are added in the frying pan with continuous sautéing.
vi. The small amount of water is added and the mix is sautéed.
vii. The grated tomatoes are added.
viii. Salt is also added and mixed.
ix. The flame is reduced to low, the lid is covered on the fry pan.
x. Let it cook for 10-15 minutes or till the Chhole get cooked and water is evaporated.
xi. The curry is transferred to the storage bowl and the minced Kothambir is added with stirring.
xii. This curry is served garnished with the onion pieces.

2. SOOKHE CHANE KI SABJI (BLACK CHANAA DRY VEG)

The ingredients and the process are as above (Chhole Dry Veg) except that black chanaa replaces the Chhole.

3. SOOKHI MATAR KI SABJI (PEAS DRY VEG)

The ingredients and the process are as above (Chhole Dry Veg) except that dry peas replace the chhole.

4. SOOKHI RAAJMAA BEANS KI SABJI (LOBIA DRY DRY VEG)

The ingredients and the process are as above (Chhole Dry Veg) except that chaulai beans replace the Chhole.

VI. SABJI-PHALON KI SOOKHI SABJI (FRUIT VEGETABLES-WITHOUT GRAVY)

1. TAMAATAR KI GAADI SABJI (TOMATO THICK CURRY)

Ingredients:

i.	Tomatoes	250 Gm
ii.	Oil	2 Tbs
iii.	Onion	½ Cup
iv.	Green chilies	1 Tbs or to taste
v.	Turmeric powder	½ Ts
vi.	Cumin seeds	1 Ts
vii.	Mustard seeds	¼ Ts
viii.	Fenugreek seeds	¼ Ts
ix.	Salt	to taste
x.	Sugar	2 Ts or to taste

Optional ingredients: The grated ginger, garlic and the coriander powder could be added.

Process:
  i.   Ingredients # iii and iv are grated.
  ii. Oil is heated in the frying pan on medium flame.

iii. Ingredients # iii to viii are added one by one and fried with continuous sautéing.
iv. The tomatoes are cut in to small pieces (about 2 cm cubes) and added in the frying pan with continuous sautéing.
v. Salt and sugar are added and mixed.
vi. The flame is reduced to low, the lid is covered on the fry pan.
vii. Let it cook for 5-7 minutes or till the maximum water is evaporated and it thickens sufficiently.
viii. The curry is transferred to the storage bowl and the minced Kothambir is added with stirring.
ix. This curry could be served with both Roti and rice preparations.

Optional processes:
There are three variations in the processing of tomatoes:

A. In this process, the Tomatoes are cut in small pieces & added.

B. In this, the Tomatoes are grated & the resultant paste is added.

C. In this process, the whole Tomatoes are boiled in water, then peeled and the pulp is mashed. This pulp is added. This process imparts thicker gravy due to part of potatoes disperse finely in the gravy. The taste is far superior.

2. *KARELAA KI SOOKHI SABJI (BITTER GOURD VEGETABLE)*

Ingredients:
i.	Bitter gourd	250 Gm
ii.	Water	as required
iii.	Oil	as required
iv.	Mustard seeds	¼ Ts
v.	Asafoetida	¼ Ts
vi.	Red chili powder	½ Ts
vii.	Turmeric powder	¼ Ts
viii.	Ajwain	¼ Ts
ix.	Salt	to taste
x.	Tamarind pulp	1 Ts
xi.	Special Garam Masala	½ Ts
xii.	Water	as required

* Liberal quantity is required for frying Arbi.

Process:
i. The bitter gourd fruits are sliced them in to smaller round pieces.
ii. The oil is heated in the Deep frying pan and mustard seeds are added.
iii. When they start crackling, the spices # v to viii are added and fried at low flame.
iv. The bitter gourd pieces are added in the Deep frying pan with the continuous mixing.
v. The tamarind pulp and Special garam masala are added and mixed.
vi. Add salt and small amount of water and cook till the bitter gourd pieces become tender and excess water is evaporated.
vii. The Dry spiced Bitter gourd Dry Veg is ready to be served.

3. BHATAA KI SOOKHI SABJI (BRINJAL DRY VEG)

Ingredients:

i.	Brinjal *(Any kind but with minimum seeds)*	250 Gm
ii.	Oil	3 Tbs
iii.	Onion	4 Tbs
iv.	Green chilies	1 Tbs or to taste
v.	Coriander powder	2 Ts
vi.	Turmeric powder	½ Ts
vii.	Cumin seeds	1½ Ts
viii.	Mustard seeds	¼ Ts
ix.	Fenugreek seeds	¼ Ts
x.	Asafoetida	¼ Ts
xi.	Salt	to taste
xii.	Kothambir	1 Tbs

Optional ingredients:
- The grated ginger, garlic and the coriander powder could be added.
- Tomatoes (½ Cup-grated) could be added.

Process:
i. Ingredients # iii and iv are grated.
ii. Oil is heated in the frying pan on medium flame.
iii. Ingredients # iii to xi are added one by one and fried with continuous sautéing.
iv. The brinjals are cut in to small pieces (about 3-4 cm cube) and placed in a bowl of water.
v. They are added in the frying pan with continuous sautéing.
vi. The salt is also added and mixed.
vii. The flame is reduced to low and the lid is covered on the fry pan.
viii. Let it cook for 8-10 minutes.
ix. The dry veg is transferred to the storage bowl and the minced Kothambir is added with stirring.
x. The Brinjal Dry Veg could be served with both Roti and rice preparations.

4. KUMRAA KI GAADI SABJI (PUMPKIN THICK CURRY)

Ingredients:
i. Pumpkin   250 Gm
ii. Oil   1 Tbs
iii. Onion   3 Tbs
iv. Green chilies   1 Tbs or to taste
v. Turmeric powder   ½ Ts
vi. Cumin seeds   1 Ts
vii. Mustard seeds   ¼ Ts
viii. Salt   to taste
ix. Sugar   2 Ts or to taste

Process:
i. Ingredients # iii and iv are grated.
ii. Oil is heated in the frying pan on medium flame.
iii. Ingredients # iii to vii are added one by one and fried with continuous sautéing.
iv. The Pumpkin is peeled and cut in to small pieces (about 2 cm cubes) and added in the frying pan with continuous sautéing.
v. Salt and sugar are added and mixed.
vi. The flame is reduced to low, the lid is covered on the fry pan.

vii. Let it cook for 8-10 minutes or till the pumpkin pieces get softened.
viii. The curry is transferred to the storage bowl and the minced Kothambir is added with stirring.
ix. This curry could be served with both Roti and rice preparations.

5. *LAUKI KI SOOKHI SOOKHI SABJI (ASH GOURD DRY VEG)*

Ingredients:
i.	Ash gourd	250 Gm
ii.	Oil	1 Tbs
iii.	Onion	3 Tbs
iv.	Green chilies	1 Tbs or to taste
v.	Turmeric powder	½ Ts
vi.	Cumin seeds	1½ Ts
vii.	Mustard seeds	¼ Ts
viii.	Salt	to taste
ix.	Kothambir	1 Tbs

Optional ingredient: Tomatoes (½ Cup, grated to paste) could be added.

Process:
i. Ingredients # iii and iv are grated.
ii. Oil is heated in the frying pan on medium flame.
iii. Ingredients # iii to vii are added one by one and fried with continuous sautéing.
iv. The ash gourd is cut in to small pieces (about 2 cm cubes) and added in the frying pan with continuous sautéing.
v. The grated tomatoes are added.
vi. Salt is also added and mixed.
vii. The flame is reduced to low, the lid is covered on the fry pan.
viii. Let it cook for 8-10 minutes or till the mix becomes homogenous.
ix. The curry is transferred to the storage bowl and the minced Kothambir is added with stirring.
x. This curry could be served with both Roti and rice preparations.

6. KAKRI KI SOOKHI SABJI (CUCUMBER DRY VEG)

The ingredients and the process are as above (Ash gourd Dry Veg) except that cucumber replaces the ash gourd.

7. PHADKULI KI SOOKHI SABJI (SMOOTH GOURD DRY VEG)

The ingredients and the process is as above (Lauki ki Sookhi Sabji) except that ash gourd is replaced by smooth gourd.

8. PHOOL-GOBHI KI SOOKHI SABJI (CAULIFLOWER DRY VEG)

Ingredients:
i.	Cauliflower	250 Gm
ii.	Oil	3 Tbs
iii.	Onion	3 Tbs
iv.	Ginger	2 Ts
v.	Garlic	2 Ts
vi.	Green chilies	1 Tbs or to taste
vii.	Coriander powder	2 Ts
viii.	Turmeric powder	½ Ts
ix.	Cumin seeds	1 Ts
x.	Tomatoes *(Grated to paste)*	½ Cup
xi.	Salt	to taste
xii.	Kothambir	1 Tbs

Process:
i. Ingredients # iii to vi are grated.
ii. Oil is heated in the frying pan on medium flame.
iii. Ingredients # iii to ix are added one by one and fried with continuous sautéing.
iv. The cauliflower is cut in to small pieces (about 2 cm size individual flower bunch) and added in the frying pan with continuous sautéing.
v. The grated tomatoes are added.

- vi. Salt is also added and mixed.
- vii. The flame is reduced to low, the lid is covered on the fry pan.
- viii. Let it cook for 8-10 minutes or till the cauliflower pieces are cooked.
- ix. The curry is transferred to the storage bowl and the minced Kothambir is added with stirring.
- x. This curry could be served with both Roti and rice preparations.

9. *PATTAA-GOBHI KI SOOKHI SABJI (CABBAGE DRY VEG)*

The ingredients and the process is as above (Cauliflower Dry Veg) except that cauliflower is replaced by cabbage.

10. *PARVAL KI SOOKHI SABJI (DRY VEG)*

Ingredients:
- i. Parval — 250 Gm
- ii. Oil — 3 Tbs
- iii. Onion — 3 Tbs
- iv. Green chilies — 1 Tbs or to taste
- v. Coriander powder — 2 Ts
- vi. Turmeric powder — ½ Ts
- vii. Cumin seeds — 1 Ts
- viii. Salt — to taste
- ix. Kothambir — 1 Tbs

Optional ingredients: The grated ginger, garlic and the coriander powder could be added.

Process:
- i. Ingredients # iii and iv are grated.
- ii. Oil is heated in the frying pan on medium flame.
- iii. Ingredients # iii to vii are added one by one and fried with continuous sautéing.
- iv. The Parval fruits are cut in to small pieces (about 1 cm size circles) and added in the frying pan with continuous sautéing.
- v. Salt is also added and mixed.
- vi. The flame is reduced to low, the lid is covered on the fry pan.

vii. Let it cook for 10-12 minutes or till the Parval pieces become soft / tender.
viii. The curry is transferred to the storage bowl and the minced Kothambir is added with stirring.
ix. This curry could be served with both Roti and rice preparations.

11. KUNDROO KI RASILI SABJI (GHERKINS)

The ingredients and the process is as above (Parval ki Sookhi Sabji) except that Parval is replaced by Kundroo.

12. KONS (MUNGAA) KI SOOKHI SABJI (DRUMSTICK DRY VEG)

Ingredients:

Drumsticks	12 pieces (2-2.5" Long)
Oil	3 Tbs
Onion	3 Tbs
Green chilies	1 Tbs or to taste
Turmeric powder	½ Ts
Cumin seeds	1½ Ts
Tomatoes	½ Cup
(Grated to paste)	
Salt	to taste
Special Garam Masala	1 Ts
Kothambir	1 Tbs
Water	as required

Optional ingredients:
The potatoes (1 Cup 2 cm cube size small pieces) could be added. The grated ginger and garlic could be added.

Process:
i. Ingredients # iii and iv are grated.
ii. Oil is heated in the frying pan on medium flame.
iii. Ingredients # iii to vi are added one by one and fried with continuous sautéing.
iv. The outer green skin of the drumsticks is peeled and they are cut in to small pieces (about 2" to 2.5" long) and added in the frying pan with continuous sautéing.

v. The water is added and the mix is sautéed. They are cooked for 10 minutes.
vi. The grated tomatoes are added.
vii. Salt is also added and mixed.
viii. The flame is reduced to low, the lid is covered on the fry pan.
ix. Let it cook for 15-20 minutes or till the drumsticks become soft / tender and excess water is evaporated.
x. The Special Garam Masala is added with mixing.
xi. The curry is transferred to the storage bowl and the minced Kothambir is added with stirring.
xii. This curry could be served with both Roti and rice preparations.

13. KACHARIYAA (WILD BRINJAL SPECIES VEG)

Ingredients
i. Kachariyaa — 250 Gm
ii. Oil (for frying) — as required
iii. Turmeric powder — ½ Ts
iv. Salt — to taste
v. Red chili powder — ½ Ts or to taste

Optional ingredients: Onion, garlic and ginger could be added.

Process:
i. The Kachariyaas are washed and (each is) cut in two equal pieces from the end to end in the middle. The seeds are taken out and discarded.
ii. Oil is heated in the fry pan, turmeric and red chili powders are added with sautéing.
iii. The Kachariyaas are added to sautéing and they are sautéed till completely fried.

VII. SOOKHI BEANS AUR CHANE KI SOOKHI SABJI (DRIED LEGUMES / BEANS DRY VEG)

1. GULAABI CHANE / CHHOLE KI SOOKHI SABJI (CHHOLE DRY VEG)

Ingredients:

i.	Chhole	250 Gm
ii.	Oil	4 Tbs
iii.	Onion	½ Cup
iv.	Ginger	1 Tbs
v.	Garlic	1 Tbs
vi.	Green chilies	2 Tbs or to taste
vii.	Coriander powder	1 Tbs
viii.	Turmeric powder	½ Ts
ix.	Cumin seeds	2 Ts
x.	Tomatoes *(Grated to paste)*	½ Cup
xi.	Salt	to taste
xii.	Special Garam Masala	2 Ts
xiii.	Kothambir	1 Tbs
xiv.	Water	as required

Process:
  i. Ingredients # iii to vi are grated.
  ii. Oil is heated in the frying pan on medium flame.
  iii. Ingredients # iii to ix are added one by one and fried with continuous sautéing.
  iv. The water is added in the Chhole and they are cooked in the pressure cooker.
  v. These softened Chhole are added in the frying pan with continuous sautéing.
  vi. Small amount of water is added and the mix is sautéed.
  vii. The grated tomatoes are added.
  viii. Salt is also added and mixed.
  ix. The flame is reduced to low, the lid is covered on the fry pan.
  x. Let it cook for 10 -15 minutes or till the excess water is evaporated.
  xi. The curry is transferred to the storage bowl and the minced Kothambir is added with stirring.
  xii. This curry is served garnished with the onion pieces.

2. SOOKHE CHANAA KI SOOKHI SABJI (BLACK CHANAA DRY VEG)

The ingredients and the process are as above (Chhole Dry Veg) except that black chanaa replaces the Chhole.

3. SOOKHE MATAR KI SOOKHI SABJI (PEAS DRY VEG)

The ingredients and the process are as above (Chhole Dry Veg) except that dry peas replace the Chhole.

4. SOOKHE CHAULAI BEANS KI SOOKHI SABJI (LOBIA BEANS DRY VEG)

The ingredients and the process are as above (Chhole Dry Veg) except that chaulai beans replace the Chhole.

VIII. TAAJE / GREEN BEANS AUR CHANE KI SOOKHI SABJI (FRESH LEGUMES / BEANS DRY VEG)

1. KACHCHE GULAABI CHANE KI SOOKHI SABJI / GREEN CHHOLE (GREEN CHHOLE DRY VEG)

Ingredients:

i.	Green Chhole	250 Gm
ii.	Oil	4 Tbs
iii.	Onion	½ Cup
iv.	Ginger	1 Tbs
v.	Garlic	1 Tbs
vi.	Green chilies	2 Tbs or to taste
vii.	Coriander powder	1 Tbs
viii.	Turmeric powder	½ Ts
ix.	Cumin seeds	2 Ts
x.	Tomatoes *(Grated to paste)*	½ Cup
xi.	Salt	to taste
xii.	Special Garam Masala	2 Ts
xiii.	Kothambir	1 Tbs
xiv.	Water	as required

Process:
i. Ingredients # iii to vi are grated.
ii. Oil is heated in the frying pan on medium flame.
iii. Ingredients # iii to ix are added one by one and fried with continuous sautéing.
iv. The green Chhole are added in the frying pan with continuous sautéing.
v. Small amount of water is added and the mix is sautéed.
vi. The grated tomatoes are added.
vii. Salt is also added and mixed.
viii. The flame is reduced to low and the lid is covered on the fry pan.
ix. Let it cook for 10 -15 minutes or till the excess water is evaporated.
x. The curry is transferred to the storage bowl and the minced Kothambir is added with stirring.
xi. This curry is served garnished with the onion pieces.

2. KACHCHE CHANE KI SOOKHI SABJI (FRESH BLACK CHANAA DRY VEG)

The ingredients and the process are as above (Green Chhole Dry Veg) except that fresh black chanaa replaces the fresh Gulaabi chanaa (green Chhole).

3. HARI MATAR KI SOOKHI SABJI (GREEN PEAS DRY VEG)

The ingredients and the process are as above (Green Chhole Dry Veg) except that fresh peas replace the fresh Gulaabi chanaa (green Chhole).

4. KACHCHE CHAULAI BEANS KI SOOKHI SABJI (RAW LOBIA BEANS DRY VEG)

The ingredients and the process are as above (Green Chhole Dry Veg) except that fresh chaulai beans replace the fresh Gulaabi chanaa (green Chhole).

C. BHARTAA (MASHED ROASTED / BOILED VEGETABLES)

1. BHUNJE ALOO KA SAADAA BHARTAA (ROASTED POTATO MASH - PLAIN)

Sufficient for 4 persons.

This is very tasty and healthy dish.

Ingredients:

i.	Potatoes (Big size)	500 Gm
ii.	Mustard seeds	¼ Ts.
iii.	Green Chilies	1 Tbs
iv.	Kothambir	1 Tbs
v.	Salt	to taste

Process:

i. The potatoes are placed on direct fire for roasting.

ii. A wire mesh may be placed on fire to avoid charring of Tomatoes, both surface and flesh.

iii. After due roasting, the potatoes are removed, cleaned and washed. Then the surface peel is removed.

iv. The flesh is collected, beaten to make uniform consistency. This is Bhartaa.

v. All the ingredients (step # iii to vii) are mixed with Bhartaa and it is beaten again to make it homogeneous in taste and consistency.

vi. It goes well with Roti dishes like Paraathaa.

2. BHUNJE ALOO KA TALAA BHARTAA (ROASTED MASHED POTATO - FRIED)

Ingredients and process before the addition of spices remain the same.

Further processing:

- The oil is heated in the deep frying pan and all the above spices are added and fried.
- Bhartaa is also added to it and mixed thoroughly.

Optional Ingredients: Garlic, Ginger and Onion.

3. UBLE ALOO KA SAADAA BHARTAA (BOILED MASHED POTATO - PLAIN)

* Sufficient for 4 persons.

This is very tasty and healthy dish.

Ingredients:

i.	Potatoes (Big size)	500 Gm
ii.	Mustard seeds	¼ Ts.
iii.	Green Chilies	1 Tbs
iv.	Kothambir	1 Tbs
v.	Salt	to taste

Process:

i. The potatoes are placed in presser cooker for cooking. They could also be boiled in the boiling water in a deep bowl, heated on medium flame.

ii. After due boiling, the potatoes are removed, cleaned and washed. Then the surface peel is removed.

iii. The flesh is collected, beaten to make uniform consistency. Some water is added if required. This is Bhartaa.

iv. All the ingredients (step # iii to vii) are mixed with Bhartaa and it is beaten again to make it homogeneous in taste and consistency.

It goes well with Roti dishes like Paraathaa.

4. UBLE ALOO KA TALAA BHARTAA (BOILED POTATO MASH - FRIED)

Ingredients and process before the addition of spices remain the same.

Further processing:

- The oil is heated in the deep frying pan and all the above spices are added and fried.
- Bhartaa is also added to it and mixed thoroughly.

Optional Ingredients: Garlic, Ginger and Onion.

5. BHUNJE BHATE KA SAADAA BHARTAA (ROASTED BRINJAL MASHED PULP - PLAIN)

* Sufficient for 4 persons.

This is very tasty and healthy dish.

Ingredients:

i.	Brinjal (Big size, Green or Violet)	500 Gm
ii.	Asafoetida	¼ Ts
iii.	Mustard seeds	¼ Ts
iv.	Green Chilies	1 Tbs
v.	Kothambir	1 Tbs
vi.	Salt	to taste
vii.	Rock salt	to taste

Process:

i. This process is recommended by Ayurveda and states that this non-fried dish alleviates all the vitiated Doshas.

ii. Several holes are made in the flesh of Brinjal on all sides and asafoetida is inserted in each hole.

iii. The Brinjal is placed on direct fire for roasting.

iv. A wire mesh may be placed on fire to avoid charring of Brinjal, both surface and flesh.

- v. After due roasting, the Brinjal is removed, cleaned and washed. Then the surface peel is removed.
- vi. The flesh is collected, beaten to make uniform consistency. This is Bhartaa.
- vii. All the ingredients (step # iii to vii) are mixed with Bhartaa and it is beaten again to make it homogeneous in taste and consistency.
- viii. It goes well with Roti dishes like Paraathaa and Gaakar.

6. BHUNJE BHATE KA TALAA BHARTAA (ROASTED BRINJAL MASHED PULP - FRIED)

Ingredients and process before the addition of spices remain the same.

Further processing:

- The oil is heated in the deep frying pan and all the above spices are added and fried.
- Bhartaa is also added to it and mixed thoroughly.

Optional Ingredients: Garlic, Ginger and Onion.

7. BHUNJE TAMAATAR KA SAADAA BHARTAA (ROASTED TOMATO MASHED PULP - PLAIN)

* Sufficient for 4 persons.

This is very tasty and healthy dish.

Ingredients:

i.	Tomatoes (Big size, Red and pulpy)	500 Gm
ii.	Mustard seeds	¼ Ts
iii.	Green Chilies	1 Tbs
iv.	Kothambir	1 Tbs
v.	Salt	to taste

Process:

i. Several holes are made in the flesh of Tomatoes on all sides, to allow the steam to escape.
ii. The Tomatoes are placed on direct fire for roasting.
iii. A wire mesh may be placed on fire to avoid charring of Tomatoes s, both surface and flesh.
iv. After due roasting, the Tomatoes are removed, cleaned and washed. Then the surface peel is removed.
v. The flesh is collected, beaten to make uniform consistency. This is Bhartaa.
vi. All the ingredients (step # iii to vii) are mixed with Bhartaa and it is beaten again to make it homogeneous in taste and consistency.
vii. It goes well with Roti dishes like Paraathaa.

8. BHUNJE TAMAATAR KA TALAA BHARTAA (ROASTED TOMATO MASHED PULP - FRIED)

Ingredients and process before the addition of spices remain the same.

Further processing:

- The oil is heated in the deep frying pan and all the above spices are added and fried.
- Bhartaa is also added to it and mixed thoroughly.

Optional Ingredients: Garlic, Ginger and Onion.

9. UBLE TOMATO KA SAADAA BHARTAA (BOILED TOMATO MASHED PULP - PLAIN)

* Sufficient for 4 persons.

This is very tasty and healthy dish.

Ingredients:

i. Tomatoes   500 Gm

   (Big size, Red and pulpy)

ii. Mustard seeds — ¼ Ts.
iii. Green Chilies — 1 Tbs
iv. Kothambir — 1 Tbs
v. Salt — to taste

Process:
i. The Tomatoes are placed in presser cooker for cooking. They could also be boiled in the boiling water in a deep bowl, heated on medium flame.
ii. After due boiling, the Tomatoes are removed, cleaned and washed. Then the surface peel is removed.
iii. The flesh is collected, beaten to make uniform consistency. This is Bhartaa.
iv. All the ingredients (step # iii to vii) are mixed with Bhartaa and it is beaten again to make it homogeneous in taste and consistency.
v. It goes well with Roti dishes like Paraathaa.

10. UBLE TOMATO KA TALAA BHARTAA (BOILED TOMATO MASHED PULP - FRIED)

Ingredients and process before the addition of spices remain the same.

Further processing:
- The oil is heated in the deep frying pan and all the above spices are added and fried.
- Bhartaa is also added to it and mixed thoroughly.

Optional Ingredients: Garlic, Ginger and Onion.

D. BHARVAA SABJI (STUFFED VEGETABLES)

In Bundelkhand, the common vegetables which are stuffed with spice-mix and then cooked are:
i. Brinjal (Baigan)
ii. Ladies finger (Bhindi)

iii. Bitter gourds (Karelaa)
iv. Coccinia indica (Kundaroo)
v. Capsicum (Shimla mirch)
vi. Parval (Trichosanthes dioica)

BHARVA MASALA: (STUFFING SPICE MIX)

The spice-mix that is stuffed inside the vertically slit vegetable fruit, consists of two parts:
    A. Stock spice mix
    B. Spot spice mix
    C. Mixing the Spice-mix A and B

The details are as under:

A. Stock spice-mix

This mix is the stock from which the required amount is withdrawn at the time of cooking the 'stuffed vegetable'.

Ingredients:
i.	Cumin seeds	2 Tbs
ii.	Fenugreek seeds	2 Tbs
iii.	Fennel seeds	2 Tbs
iv.	Mustard seeds	1 Tbs
v.	Coriander seeds	½ Cup

Process:
i. All the five spices are roasted individually.
ii. They are ground to coarse powder and mixed well.

B. Spot spice mix

This spice mix is to be prepared at the time of cooking the 'stuffed vegetable'.

Ingredients:
i. Asafoetida   Equal to 2 wheat grains

ii.	Oil	as required to fry (i)
iii.	Ginger	1 Ts
iv.	Garlic	1 Ts
v.	Green chilies	1 Tbs
vi.	Amchur	1 Ts
	(Dry raw mango powder)	

Process:
- The Asafoetida is fried in minimum quantity of oil and ground.
- The other ingredients # iii to v are grated and # vi is mixed with them.

C. Mixing the Spice-mix A and B

Ingredients:
i.	Spice-mix A	1 part
ii.	Spice-mix B	1 part
iii.	Oil	1½ Part

Optional ingredients: Mash of one medium size Boiled potato to increase the bulk and adhesiveness of the final stuffing spice-mix.

Process:
i. The equal parts of both the spice-mixes A and B are added together and mixed.
ii. The oil (150% of one spice mix) is added to above mix.
iii. The final blend is mixed thoroughly to get uniform spice mix.

Preparation of the Stuffed Vegetables

Ingredients:
i.	The vegetable *(Anyone of above listed)*	250 Gm
ii.	Stuffing Spice mix	2 Tbs
iii.	Oil for frying	2 Tbs
iv.	Salt	to taste
v.	Kothambir (Minced)	1 Tbs
vi.	Red chili powder	to taste
vii.	Turmeric powder	½ Ts

Process:
i. The vegetable fruits are washed and air dried.
ii. They are slit vertically in the middle from near top to near bottom, by a sharp knife. The fruits remain firmly joined.
iii. The Stuffing spice mix is filled in the slit of the fruits.
iv. Oil is heated in the frying pan, the turmeric powder is added with sautéing and then these spice filled fruits are placed on the hot oil one by one.
v. The pan is covered and cooking is continued.
vi. After five minutes salt and the red chili powder are added with sautéing and cooking is continued.
vii. When they are cooked, Kothambir mince is added.
viii. The Stuffed Vegetable is ready to be served.

E. CHHILKON KI SOOKHI SABJIYAA (DRY VEG OF PEEL / SKIN OF VEGETABLES)

1. KARELAA CHHILKAA KI SOOKHI SABJI (DRY VEG OF GREEN PEELS BITTER GOURD)

This vegetable is full of bitter principles which are healthy but taste is very bitter. One has to overcome the dislike of bitter taste in order to get health benefits.

Ingredients:

i.	Green peels of bitter gourd	100 Gm
ii.	Oil	as required
iii.	Onion*	2 Tbs
iv.	Garlic*	1 Ts
v.	Ginger*	2 Ts
vi.	Amchur *(Dried raw mango powder)*	2 Ts
vii.	Turmeric	½ Ts

viii.	Mustard seeds	¼ Ts
ix.	Green chili*	1 Tbs
x.	Salt	to taste
xi.	Special Garam Masala	½ Ts

* Grated

Optional ingredients:

Tomato could be added if desired so.

Process:

i. The oil is heated in the deep frying pan and all the spices are added (step ii to viii) and fried.

ii. Green peels of bitter gourd are added to it and mixed. Salt is added and mixed. Special Garam masala is also added and mixed.

iii. It is cooked uniformly for few minutes.

iv. Karelaa Chhilkaa Dry Sabji is ready.

v. This is served best with Roti preparation.

F. DANTHAL KI SOOKHI SABJI (DRY VEG OF STEMS OF VEGETABLES)

1. GOBHI-PHOOL EVAM PATTA-GOBHI KE DANTHAL KI SOOKHI SABJI (DRY VEG OF STEMS OF CAULIFLOWER AND CABBAGE)

This dish is full of edible fire hence cleanses the whole alimentary canal.

Ingredients:

i.	Stem of Cauliflower and/or Cabbage**	100 Gm
ii.	Onion*	2 Tbs
iii.	Garlic*	½ Ts
iv.	Ginger*	1 Ts

v.	Turmeric	½ Ts
vi.	Mustard seeds	¼ Ts
vii.	Green chili*	1 Tbs
viii.	Salt	to taste
ix.	Special Garam Masala	½ Ts
x.	Oil	as required
xi.	Water	as required

* Grated

** Cut or Diced in small pieces.

Optional ingredients:

Tomato could be added if desired so.

Process:

i. The oil is heated in the deep frying pan and all the spices are added (step ii to vii) and fried.

ii. The diced small pieces of the stem(s) of Cauliflower and / or Cabbage are added to it and mixed. Salt is added and mixed. Special Garam masala is added and mixed.

iii. About 2 Tbs water is sprinkled on it and lid is covered.

iv. It is cooked uniformly for few minutes.

v. The Cauliflower / Cabbage ke danthal ki Sookhi Sabji is ready. This is served with Roti preparation.

G. SOOKHI PATTAA BHAAJI (LEAFY VEGETABLE DRY)

1. METHI BHAALI (FENUGREEK LEAVES DRY VEG)

2. PAALAK BHAAJI (SPINACH LEAVES DRY VEG)

3. CHAULAI BHAAJI (PRICKLY AMARANTH DRY VEG)

4. MOORAA KE PATTO KI BHAAJI (RADISH LEAVES DRY VEG)

5. SARSO KE PATTO KI BHAAJI (MUSTARD LEAVES DRY VEG)

6. GHUIYAA KE PATTE KI BHAAJI (COLOCASIA LEAVES DRY VEG)

7. GOBHI KE PATTE KI BHAAJI (CAULIFLOWER LEAVES DRY VEG)

8. PARVAL KE PATTE KI BHAAJI (TRICHOSANTHES DIOICA LEAVES DRY VEG)

9. GILOY KE PATTE KI BHAAJI (TINOSPORA LEAVES DRY VEG)

10. MAKUIYYAA KE PATTON KI BHAAJI (GREEN LEAVES OF MAKUIYYAA)

The leaves are taken from the shrub that bears red fruits and not the black ones.

For each of the 10 above, the basic ingredients and cooking process is common to all and given below:

Ingredients:
i.	Leafy vegetable minced *(Any one from the ten above)*	2 Cups
ii.	Onion*	½ Cup
iii.	Garlic*	½ Ts
iv.	Ginger*	½ Ts
v.	Green chili*	2 Ts
vi.	Oil	2 Tbs
vii.	Salt	to taste

* Grated

Process:
i. Oil is heated in the fry pan on slow flame.
ii. The onion is added and fried with continuous sautéing.
iii. The green chili, ginger and garlic are added and fried with continuous sautéing.

iv. The minced green leaves of the chosen Vegetable (Out of 1 to 9 listed above) are added in the mix with continuous sautéing.
v. The salt is added with mixing.
vi. The lid is placed on the pan and it is cooked on slow flame for 5-8 minutes.
vii. The Leafy vegetable Dry Sabji is ready.

H. AALOO VAALI SOOKHI BHAAJI (LEAFY VEGETABLE WITH POTATOES DRY SABJI)

1. METHI AALOO BHAALI (POTATO FENUGREEK LEAVES DRY VEG)

2. AALOO PAALAK BHAAJI (POTATO SPINACH LEAVES DRY VEG)

3. AALOO CHAULAI BHAAJI (POTATO PRICKLY AMARANTH DRY VEG)

4. AALOO GHUIYAA KE PATTE KI BHAAJI (COLOCASIA LEAVES DRY VEG)

5. AALOO GOBHI KE PATTE KI BHAAJI (POTATO CAULIFLOWER LEAVES DRY VEG)

6. PARVAL KE PATTE KI BHAAJI (TRICHOSANTHES DIOICA LEAVES DRY VEG)

7. GILOY KE PATTE KI BHAAJI (TINOSPORA LEAVES DRY VEG)

For each of the above, the basic ingredients and cooking process is common to all and given below:

Ingredients:
i. Leafy vegetable Minced   2 Cups
   (Any one of 1 to 7 above)
ii. Onion*   ½ Cup.

iii.	Garlic*	½ Ts
iv.	Ginger*	½ Ts
v.	Green chili*	2 Ts
vi.	Oil	2 Tbs
vii.	Salt	to taste
viii.	Potatoes	2 Cups

(Cut in small 2 cm square pieces)

* Grated

Process:
i. Oil is heated in the fry pan on slow flame.
ii. The onion is added and fried with continuous sautéing.
iii. The green chili, ginger and garlic are added and fried with continuous sautéing.
iv. The potato pieces are added and fried with continuous sautéing.
v. The minced green leaves of the chosen Vegetable (Out of 1 to 7 listed above) are added in the mix with continuous sautéing.
vi. The salt is added with mixing.
vii. The lid is placed on the pan and it is cooked on slow flame for 5-8 minutes.
viii. The Leafy vegetable Dry Sabji is ready.

CHAPTER 6: DAARE / DAAL (LENTILS AS CURRY)

In Bundelkhand, the most common lentil used (as accompaniment to Roti and Rice preparations) is Pigeon pea / Yellow Lentil i.e. Tuar Daal, locally called Raahar Daal or Arhar Daal.

The second place is occupied by Green gram i.e. Moong Daal. Black gram is also in use but less frequently.

There are several kinds of Daal (as curry) preparations viz.

1. Saadi Daal (Plain cooking)
2. Baghaari Daal (With Baghaar application)
3. Khaas Baghaari Daal (Daal Fried nee Daal Fry / Daal Tadkaa)
4. Mili-Juli Daal (Mixed lentils)
5. Bhaaji Daal

1. SAADI DAAR (PLAIN LENTIL AS CURRY)

This forms part of staple food along with Roti and Bhaat (Cooked rice).

Ingredients:

i.	Pigeon pea	2 Cups
ii.	Water	3 Cup or as required
iii.	Turmeric powder	½ Ts
iv.	Salt	to taste
v.	Ghee	as required

Process:

i. The pigeon pea is placed in the pressure cooker vessel. The required quantity of water is added.
ii. Salt and turmeric powder are added in it.
iii. It is cooked as per standard operation.
iv. It is served by garnishing with Ghee. (Generally one Ts per cup Daal)

2. BAGHAARI DAAL

Originally an earthen lamp (Diyaa) like the one lighted on Diwali festival, is used for the application of Baghaar. The Ghee is heated in such earthen Diyaa, held by a tong. All the spices are added in it. The Diyaa is heated further, on the direct flame, till it become red hot and smoking. Then this Diyaa is dipped in the Dall and the lid is covered.

One should be careful as the flames and smoke come out rapidly when the red hot Diyaa (and the smoking spices in it) touch the Daal.

Ingredients:

i.	Plain Daal (from 1)	4 Cup
ii.	Ghee	1 Tbs
iii.	Asafoetida	Equal to small pea size
iv.	Cumin seeds	½ Ts
v.	Red chilly powder	1 Ts or to taste
vi.	Mustard seeds	¼ Ts

Process: As above but the steel spatula of appropriate size could be used.

3. KHAAS BAGHAARI DAAL (DAAL FRIED NEE DAAL FRY / DAAL TADKAA)

This Baghaar is applied in the Kadai or deep fry pan only as the quantum of ingredients is quite high.

Ingredients:

i.	Plain Daal (from 1)	4 Cup
ii.	Ghee	2 Tbs
iii.	Asafoetida	Equal to small pea size
iv.	Cumin seeds	½ Ts
v.	Red chili powder	1 Ts or to taste
vi.	Mustard seeds	¼ Ts
vii.	Tomato	½ Cup
viii.	Onion	¼ Cup
ix.	Garlic	2 Ts
x.	Ginger	2 Ts

| xi. | Bay leaves (Curry patta) | 6 *(Broken in 1" long pieces)* |

Process:

i. The Ghee is heated in a deep frying pan on medium flame.
ii. The asafetida, onion, garlic and ginger are added one by one in the hot Ghee with sautéing and fried.
iii. The bay leaves are added and fried.
iv. The cumin seeds, mustard seeds and red chili powder are added with sautéing.
v. The flame is increased to high and the Plain Daal is added and the lid of the fry pan is covered. It is cooked for 2-3 minutes.
vi. The Khaas Baghaari Daal is ready to be served.
vii. It goes well with Roti as well as Rice preparations.

4. *MILI-JULI DAAL (MIXED LENTILS CURRY)*

Ingredients:

i.	Pigeon pea (Tuar)	1 Cup
ii.	Green gram (Moong)	1 Cup
iii.	Black gram (Urad)	1 Cup
iv.	Turmeric powder	½ Ts
v.	Salt	to taste
vi.	Ghee	as required

Process:

i. The three daals are placed in the pressure cooker vessel. The required quantity of water is added.
ii. Salt and turmeric powder are added in it.
iii. It is cooked as per standard operation.
iv. It is served by garnishing with Ghee. (Generally one Ts per cup Daal)

Optional dishes:

- This Mixed Dall could be fried like Baghaari Daal.
- This Mixed Dall could be fried like Khaas Baghaari Daal.

5. DARR BHAAJIYAA (COOKED WITH LEAFY VEG)

1. PAALAK DAAR-BHAJIYAA (PIGEONPEA CURRY WITH SPINACH)

This Daal is tasty and healthy combination of the protein and iron.

* **Sufficient for 4 persons.**

Ingredients:

i.	Pigeon pea (Tuar Daal)	150 Gm
ii.	Fenugreek (Methi)* leaves	4 Tbs
iii.	Spinach (Paalak)* leaves	4 Tbs
iv.	(Chaulai) Prickly Amaranthus leaves*	4 Tbs
v.	Water	as required
vi.	Oil	as required
vii.	Asafoetida	¼ Ts
viii.	Lovage (Ajwain)	¼ Ts
ix.	Turmeric powder	¼ Ts
x.	Mustard seeds	¼ Ts
xi.	Salt	to taste
xii.	Tomato (Medium size)	1

Optional ingredients:

* Out of three vegetables, all three, any two or anyone could be added. Any other leafy vegetable could also be used.

Process:

i. The pigeon pea and the leafy vegetables (Chopped finely) are washed and loaded in the cooker with requisite amount of water. Salt is added. They are cooked.

ii. They are mixed properly.

   iii. The small quantity of Ghee is heated in Deep frying pan and Asafoetida and Mustard seeds are added, followed by Ajwain and Turmeric powder. The mix is sautéed.

   iv. The cooked Pigeon pea and leafy vegetables mixture is poured in the deep frying pan and mixed.

   v. The tomato is grated and added in the same.

   vi. It is continuously mixed while heating.

Rasili Daar Bhajiyaa is ready to be served with plain rice and Roti.

2. MUNGAA PHOOL DAAR BHAAJIYAA (DRUMSTCK FLOWERS COOKED IN PIGEON PEA)

This Tuar lentil dish has pleasant consistency, feel and flavor.

* Sufficient for 3 persons.

Ingredients:

i.	Pigeon pea	150 Gm
ii.	Drumstick flowers	40 Gm
iii.	Water	as required
iv.	Ghee	as required
v.	Fenugreek seeds	15
vi.	Cumin seeds	½ Ts
vii.	Turmeric powder	¼ Ts
viii.	Mustard seeds	¼ Ts
ix.	Salt	to taste

Process:

   i. The pigeon pea and the drumstick flowers are washed and loaded in the cooker with requisite amount of water. Salt is added. They are cooked.

   ii. The small quantity of Ghee is heated in Deep frying pan and Mustard seeds and Fenugreek seeds are added. When they are crackling, Cumin seeds and Turmeric powder are added and fried.

iii. The cooked Pigeon pea and drumstick flowers mixture is poured in the Deep frying pan and mixed.

iv. It is continuously mixed while heating.

v. Mungaa Phool ki Raahar Daar is ready to be served with plain rice and Paraathaas.

CHAPTER 7: BARI CURRIES

1. RASILLI BARI (BARI CURRY):

* Sufficient for 2 persons.

Ingredients:

i.	Black gram Bari *or* Green gram Bari	100 Gm
ii.	Oil	as required
iii.	Asafoetida	¼ Ts
iv.	Cumin seeds	½ Ts
v.	Onion*	3 Tbs
vi.	Garlic*	½ Ts
vii.	Ginger*	1 Ts
viii.	Mustard seeds	¼ Ts
ix.	Green Chili*	1 Tbs or to taste
x.	Tomato (Medium)	2
xi.	Salt	to taste
xii.	Kothambir	1 Tbs
xiii.	Water	as required

* (Minced finely)

Optional ingredient: Potato could be cut in to small pieces and added (Also 100 Gm).

Process:

i. The Bari pieces are fried in the Oil and kept aside.
ii. Oil is heated in the Deep frying pan and Onion, Garlic, Cumin seeds, Mustard seeds and green Chilies are fried.
iii. The fried Bari pieces are added to it and mixed. Salt is added.
iv. Water is added, mixed and the mix is simmered on low flame.
v. When Bari pieces are cooked, the pre-fried asafetida is added. Ginger is also added. The cooking is continued.

vi.	The tomato is grated and added to the curry and cooking is continued.
vii.	Finally the Kothambir are added and mixed.

The Rasili Bari is ready and could be served with Rice, Paraathaa, Poorie or Roti.

2. BIJORAA CURRY (BARI LIKE PREPARATION CONTAINING SOME SEEDS ALSO):

This dish is prepared exactly the way of 'Bari curry', using Bijoraa instead of Bari.

CHAPTER 8: BESAN KI SOOKHI SABJIYAA (CHICKPEA FLOUR BASED DRY VEG)

1. LAPTAA:

This is the simplest to prepare yet very tasty dish to eat with white Rice and Rotis.

* Sufficient for 4 persons.

Ingredients:

i.	Besan (Chickpea flour)	200 Gm
ii.	Water	600 ml
iii.	Salt	to taste
iv.	Oil	3 Tbs
v.	Asafoetida	¼ Ts
vi.	Lovage (Ajwain)	¼ Ts
vii.	Mustard seeds	¼ Ts
viii.	Green Chili (Finely minced)	1 Tbs

Optional ingredients: Garlic and Ginger

Process:

i. In a vessel Besan & water are mixed with continuous stirring.

ii. The mix is kept aside for 2 hours to swell.

iii. Oil is heated in a Deep frying pan and Mustard seeds plus asafetida are added and sautéed till fried.

iv. Lovage and green Chilies are also added and stirred.

v. The Besan mix, from step ii, is poured in the Deep frying pan with continuous mixing at high flame.

vi. It is cooked for 15-20 minutes with continuous stirring till it thickens so much that if a finger is dipped in it and taken out, it does not fall (Hence the name Laptaa, remains embraced to the finger).

Laptaa is ready. It is tasty accomplice to white rice and plain Roti (without Ghee).

2. LAPTAA GUTTAA KI SOOKHI SABJI (SQUARE PIECES OF BESAN DRY VEG):

* **Sufficient for 4 persons.**

   i. **Ingredients and process same as per Laptaa up to this point.**
   ii. The Laptaa paste is continued to be heated till it starts bubbling (Steam bubbles escape from the surface).
   iii. Some drops of oil are placed on a Thaali (flat surfaced steel plate) and rubbed all over the area.
   iv. The thick Laptaa is poured on this Thaali and spread uniformly all over. It is left to dry (Air drying).
   v. When Laptaa is toughened, the **square pieces** are cut with aid of knife (called Laptaa Gutta).

Further processing:

Laptaa Guttaa are used to prepare Besan Gutta Sabji and Bhaaporaa.

3. BESAN GUTTA KI SOOKHI SABJI:

Ingredients:

i.	Oil	as needed
ii.	Onion	2 Tbs
iii.	Garlic	½ Ts
iv.	Ginger	1 Ts
v.	Turmeric	¼ Ts
vi.	Mustard seeds	¼ Ts
vii.	Salt	to taste

Process:

   i. The oil is heated in the Deep frying pan and all the spices are added (step ii to vi) and fried.
   ii. Laptaa Guttas are added to it and mixed. Salt is added, mixed.
   iii. It is cooked uniformly for few minutes.

iv. Laptaa Gutta ki Sookhi Sabji is ready. This is served by itself also and savoured like salty dish. It is tasty accompaniment to any rice and Roti preparation.

4. BHAAPORAA

Ingredients and process remain same till the Laptaa Guttas are cut as square pieces from the plate.

Further Processing:

Originally an earthen pitcher was filled with water and its mouth was covered with a muslin cloth. The Laptaa Guttas are placed on this muslin cloth. The pitcher was heated on the fire and the steam would pass through the muslin cloth. The steam would cook the Laptaa Guttas. The same should be turned over so that all surfaces are cooked. **(We could use the steel vessel in place of earthen pitcher).**

Ingredients:

i.	Oil	as needed
ii.	Onion	2 Tbs
iii.	Garlic	½ Ts
iv.	Ginger	1 Ts
v.	Turmeric	¼ Ts
vi.	Mustard seeds	¼ Ts
vii.	Salt	to taste

Process:

i. The oil is heated in the Deep frying pan and all the spices are added (step ii to vi) and fried.

ii. The steam-cooked Laptaa Guttas are added to it and mixed. Salt is added and mixed.

iii. It is cooked uniformly for few minutes.

The Bhapooraa are ready to be served with Chatni of choice.

CHAPTER 9: DAHI AUR MATHAA KA RASILAA KHAANAA
(CURD AND BUTTERMILK CURRIES)

A. BUNDELI KADIS:

1. BHAJIYAA KI KADI:

This is very healthy dish as it is prepared with original buttermilk which contains Lactobacillus, the beneficial bacteria, needed for the body. It has very pleasant and appetizing flavor, characteristic of both the original buttermilk and the Asafoetida.

* **Sufficient for 6 persons.**

a. Kadi gravy:

Ingredients:

i.	Besan (Chickpea flour)	200 Gm
ii.	Turmeric Powder	½ Ts
iii.	Red Chili powder	½ Ts
iv.	Cumin seeds	½ Ts
v.	Mustard seeds	¼ Ts
vi.	Salt	to taste
vii.	Special Garam Masala	½ Ts
viii.	Red Chili whole	6
ix.	Asafoetida	½ Ts
x.	Buttermilk (Preferably original)*	600 ml
xi.	Oil	as required
xii.	Water	as required

* **Optional ingredient:** The Curd, diluted with equal amount of water, could be used in place of Buttermilk if the original buttermilk is not available.

Process:

i. Add water to the Besan to make thin batter.
ii. Take oil in deep frying pan, heat it and add ingredients # ii to ix except # vi and vii and fry. When the color of red Chilies darkens and cumin seeds split, add the batter in the oil with continuous sautéing.
iii. Add Buttermilk in the above mix with continuous sautéing.
iv. Continue heating, with sautéing. , to bring the mix to boiling.
v. Then reduce the flame and let it simmer for 5-10 minutes till it achieves thicker consistency. Add salt and Special Garam Masala and sauté.

b. Bhajiyaa:

Ingredients:

i.	Besan (Chickpea flour)	150 Gm
ii.	Turmeric Powder	¼ Ts
iii.	Salt	to taste
iv.	Special Garam Masala	¼ Ts
v.	Ground oil	as required
vi.	Water	as required

Optional ingredient: Sodium bi carbonate could be added to the batter to make Bhajiyaa fluffier.

Process:

i. Take ingredients # i to vi in a vessel and mix.
ii. Add water in the above mix with continuous mixing to make a batter of thick consistency.
iii. Allow the batter to rest for 15 minutes.
iv. Then it should be beaten till it becomes fluffy.
v. In the meanwhile, oil is heated in a Deep frying pan for deep frying the Bhajiyaa.
vi. Drop the batter, in small amounts, all around in the Deep frying pan to make Bhajiyaa. Allow them to fry deeply to turn golden brown.

vii. The flame is reduced and the Bhajiyaa are turned over so that the other side is also cooked properly.

viii. Scoop out the Bhajiyaa from the oil.

c. Kadi: The hot Bhajiyaa are dropped into hot water for a minute and then taken out and drop in the heated Kadi gravy in step # vii, on the other stove (a).

Kadi is ready and should be served with white rice or plain Rotis (Without Ghee).

2. MANGORAA KI KADI (GREENGRAM'S SMALL BHAJIYAA):

In Bundelkhand the Kadi is prepared using several basic ingredients. Amongst the most popular ones are the Bhajiyaa (prepared from chickpea flour / Besan) and small size Mangori (prepared from green gram flour / Moong).

* Sufficient for 6 persons.

This is prepared in three stages:

a. Preparation of Mangoraa

b. Preparation of Kadi gravy

c. Preparation of Kadi

The details are as under:

a. Mangoraa:

Ingredients:

i.	Green gram peeled (Moong)	200 Gm
ii.	Water	as required
iii.	Salt	to taste
iv.	Ginger	2 Ts
v.	Kothambir	1 Tbs
vi.	Green chili	1 Tbs
vii.	Oil for frying	as required

Process:

i. Green gram is washed and soaked in water overnight.

ii.	It is grinded in the morning to form a thick batter.
iii.	(Half of this batter is kept aside to make the Kari gravy)
iv.	Salt is added and mixed.
v.	The grated ginger, minced green chili and Kothambir is mixed in the batter.
vi.	The oil is heated in a Deep frying pan for deep frying the Mangoraas.
vii.	Drop the batter, in small amounts, all around in the oil (Deep frying pan) to make Mangoraas.
viii.	Allow them to fry deeply to turn golden brown. The flame is reduced and the Mangoraas are turned over so that the other side is also cooked properly.
ix.	Scoop out the Mangoraas from the oil.

b. Kadi gravy:

Ingredients:

i.	Batter (reserved from step ii of a)	
ii.	Turmeric Powder	½ Ts
iii.	Red Chili powder	½ Ts
iv.	Cumin seeds	½ Ts
v.	Mustard seeds	¼ Ts
vi.	Salt	To taste
vii.	Special Garam Masala	½ Ts
viii.	Red Chili whole	6
ix.	Asafoetida	½ Ts
x.	Buttermilk (Preferably original)	600 ml
xi.	Oil	as required
xii.	Water	as required

Optional ingredient: The Curd, diluted with equal amount of water, could be used in place of Buttermilk if the original buttermilk is not available.

Process:

i.	Add water to the batter to make it thinner.
ii.	Take oil in Deep frying pan, heat it and add ingredients # ii to ix except # vi and vii and fry. When the color of red Chilies

  darkens and cumin seeds split, add the batter in the oil with continuous sautéing.
- iii. Add Buttermilk in the above mix with continuous sautéing.
- iv. Continue heating, with sautéing, to bring the mix to boiling.
- v. Then reduce the flame and let it simmer for 5-10 minutes till it achieves thicker consistency. Add salt and Special Garam Masala and sauté.

c. Kadi:

The hot Mangoraas are dropped into hot water for a minute and then taken out and drop in the heated Kadi gravy in step # vii of b.

Kadi is ready and should be served with white rice or plain Rotis (Without Ghee).

3. *MASAALEDAAR CHEELAA KI KADI (KADI OF SPICED CHEELAA):*

The preparation of Masaledar Cheelaa is given under chapter heading 'Snacks'.

The Masaledar Cheelaa is cut in to square or rectangular pieces of about 1" to 1½" in size.

These pieces are added in place of Mangoraas in the above preparation (Mangoraa ki Kadi) and 'Masaledar Cheelaa Ki Kadi' is ready.

4. *KONS KI KADI (DRUMSTICKS KADI):*

* Sufficient for 6 persons.

Ingredients:

i.	Besan (Chickpea flour)	200 Gm
ii.	Turmeric Powder	½ Ts
iii.	Red Chili powder	½ Ts
iv.	Cumin seeds	½ Ts
v.	Mustard seeds	¼ Ts
vi.	Salt	To taste
vii.	Special Garam Masala	½ Ts
viii.	Red Chili (whole)	6
ix.	Asafoetida	½ Ts
x.	Buttermilk	600 ml
xi.	Oil	as required

| xii. | Water | as required |
| xiii. | Khedaa stem pieces (2"-3" long) | 12-15 |

Process:

Part A:

i. The drumsticks peeled to remove the green fibrous cover. They are washed thoroughly.
ii. They are cut in to 2 to 3 inches long pieces.
iii. Store them separately in a bowl to be added to Kadi base.

Part B:

i. Add water to the Besan to make thin batter.
ii. ii. Take oil in deep frying pan, heat it and add ingredients # ii to ix except # vi and vii and fry.
iii. When the color of red Chilies darkens and cumin seeds split, add the batter in the oil with continuous sautéing.
iv. Add Buttermilk in the above mix with continuous sautéing. .
v. Continue heating, with sautéing, to bring the mix to boiling.

Part C:

i. Add the drumstick pieces from Part A step iv to this Kadi base.
ii. Place the lid on pan, continue heating and let it simmer for 10-15 minutes till the stems pieces are softened and the Kadi achieves thicker consistency.
iii. Add salt and Special Garam Masala and sauté.

'Kons ki Kadi' is ready to be served with bread or rice preparations.

5. KONS PHOOL KI KADI (DRUMSTICKS FLOWERS KADI)

The flowers of Drumstick are added in place of Drumstick pieces in the above preparation and 'Kons Phool Ki Kadi' is ready.

6. LAPTAA GUTTE KI KADI

The preparation of 'Laptaa Gutta ki Sookhi Sabji' is given under chapter heading 'Sookhi Sabjiyaa'.

The Laptaa Gutta is cut in to square or rectangular pieces of about 1" to 1½" in size.

These pieces are added in place of Mangoraas in the above preparation (Mangoraa ki Kadi) and 'Gutte Ki Kadi' is ready.

7. NAMKEEN JALEBI KADI (KADI OF SALTY JALEBI)
The Salty Jalebi Preparation:
Ingredients:

i.	Besan *(Chickpea flour)*	1 Cup
ii.	Water	as required
iii.	Salt	to taste
iv.	Oil	as required

Process:
The coconut device (Controlled liquid dropping system):

A special device is prepared from the coconut shell. The empty shell of the coconut is cut from the middle. The lower bowl has 2-3 ''Eyes'' (Round dark colored spots). One 'eye' is pierced to make the hole.

i. The water is added in the Besan and it is mixed thoroughly. This batter should be thinner than what is used for Bhajiyaa.
ii. Salt is added and mixed.
iii. Heat the oil in a Deep frying pan.
iv. Fill the coconut device with Besan batter. One finger should block the bottom hole.
v. The Besan batter is dropped in the hot oil in thin stream, making the formation / design of Jalebi.
vi. When they cooked well, take them out and store in separate vessel.

Kadi:

These Salty Jalebis are added in place of Mangoraas in the above preparation (Mangoraa ki Kadi) and 'Namkeen Jalebi Ki Kadi' is ready.

8. AAMARIYAA / AAMLAA KI KADI (KADI OF INDIAN GOOSEBERRY)

This does not contain buttermilk or curd. This is very healthy dish as it is full of Anti-oxidants hence Anti-aging.

* Sufficient for 4 persons.

Ingredients:

i.	Dry Indian gooseberry (Sookhaa Aamlaa)	50 Gm
ii.	Oil	as required
iii.	Chickpea flour (Besan)	200 Gm
iv.	Onion*	2 Tbs
v.	Ginger*	1 Ts
vi.	Garlic*	1 Ts
vii.	Turmeric Powder	½ Ts
viii.	Cumin seeds	½ Ts
ix.	Asafoetida	¼ Ts
x.	Mustard seeds	¼ Ts
xi.	Salt	to taste
xii.	Red Chili powder	to taste
xiii.	Water	600 ml

Optional ingredients:

* These are optional ingredients and could be deleted if so desired.

Process:

i. Small quantity of oil is taken in Deep frying pan and heated.
ii. The dry Aamlaa cloves / pieces are fried in it.
iii. The fried Aamlaa pieces are grinded to powder form using mixer.
iv. Again small quantity of oil is taken in Deep frying pan and heated.
v. Mustard seeds, Asafoetida, turmeric powder, cumin seeds, minced onion, ginger and garlic and red Chili powder are fried in the hot oil.
vi. Water is mixed with Besan to form a suspension of medium consistency.
vii. The Aamlaa powder is added to this suspension with constant stirring.
viii. This mixture is poured in the Deep frying pan containing the fried spices.

ix. The salt is added to this Aamarayaa and mixed.
x. It is cooked to the boiling point. Then the flame is reduced and the Aamarayaa is allowed to simmer for 10-15 minutes.

Aamarayaa is ready to be served. It is best served with plain white rice.

9. HINGORAA / HING KI KADI (KADI OF ASAFOETIDA)

This does not contain buttermilk or curd.

Due to Asafoetida and Besan, it is a good appetizer and could be used as soup.

Sufficient for 4 persons.

Ingreditents:

i.	Chickpea flour (Besan)	200 Gm
ii.	Asafoetida	¼ Ts
iii.	Oil	as required
iv.	Turmeric Powder	½ Ts
v.	Cumin seeds	½ Ts
vi.	Mustard seeds	¼ Ts
vii.	Salt	to taste
viii.	Green Chilies	to taste
ix.	Water	600 ml

Process:

i. Small quantity of oil is taken in Deep frying pan and heated.
ii. Mustard seeds, Asafoetida, turmeric powder, cumin seeds, green Chili are fried in the oil.
iii. Water is mixed with Besan to form a suspension of medium consistency.
iv. This mixture is poured in the Deep frying pan containing the fried spices.
v. The salt is added to this Hingoraa and mixed.
vi. It is cooked to the boiling point. Then the flame is reduced and the Hingoraa is allowed to simmer for 10-15 minutes.

Hingoraa is ready to be served. It is best served with plain white rice and Roti.

SPECIAL GARAM MASALA

Ingredients:

i.	Fennel *(Saunf)*	2 Cups
ii.	Cumin seeds *(Jeeraa)*	½ Cup
iii.	Black pepper *(Kaali Mirch)*	¼ Cup
iv.	Long peeper *(Landy pippal)*	¼ Cup
v.	Cardamom seeds *(Dondaa Ilaychi)*	2 Ts
vi.	Nutmeg *(Jaiphal)*	2Ts
vii.	Cloves *(Medium)* *(Laung / Lavang)*	25
viii.	Cinnamon bark small pieces *(Daal-chini)*	¼ Cup
ix.	Bay leaf *(Medium)* *(Tej-patta)*	20
x.	Dry ginger (Sonth)	2 Tbs
xi.	Stone flower *(Patthar phool)*	

Process:
 i. The Cumin seeds and Fennel are roasted and then pulverized in coarse powder.
 ii. The other ingredients are all pulverized as coarse powder.

Made in the USA
Coppell, TX
06 July 2022